ALSO BY FRANK LENTRICCHIA

THE
EDGE
OF
NIGHT

THE
EDGE
OF
NIGHT

Frank Lentricchia

Random House
New York

Portions of this book were first published in *Harper's, The Irish Review,* and *Raritan.*

Library of Congress Cataloging-in-Publication Data
Lentricchia, Frank.
    The edge of night/Frank Lentricchia.
        p. cm.
    ISBN 0-679-43072-5
    1. Lentricchia, Frank.   2. English teachers—United States—
Autobiography.   3. Critics—United States—Autobiography.   4. Italian
Americans—Autobiography.   I. Title.
PE64.L46A3   1994
801'.95—dc20   93-25410
[B]

Book design by Tanya M. Pérez

Manufactured in the United States of America
98765432
First Edition

For Don DeLillo

. . . a character really has his own life, marked with his own characteristics, by virtue of which he is always someone. Whereas a man . . . a man can be no one. —PIRANDELLO

September 1992

Even you don't know what you meant by you.
—*RAGING BULL*

Christmas season 1987, give or take a year. I can't remember exactly. Hillsborough, North Carolina. A kitchen. Three real people, who must not be called characters, though that's what they, along with all the other real people, must become. A woman, about seventy; her son, her son-the-author, late forties; his wife, late thirties. The older woman (the mother, the visiting mother-in-law) speaks, directing most of it to the non-Italian-American daughter-in-law, but all the time keeping the son in view, occasionally shooting him a challenging glance or remark. Her mood is better than you think; her mood is better than she thinks. She speaks as if the conversation has been rolling for some time. In fact, her words inaugurate it:

"But what I want to know is why are we so involved, because they'll never change. Change? With us? Change my ass. I have to ask you something. What kind of a look do you call that on my son's face? He's just like his father. And his father is just like *his* father, that's where it all comes from, but my husband's father was the worst. He's the one who scared me. With their friends they're different, then they change in a hurry. My father-in-law was so cold you don't even know what I mean by 'cold.' I was ashamed to smoke, he never said a word and I was ashamed. You think I don't notice your husband when you smoke? I notice everything. And what are you looking at? What is he looking at? Naturally your husband is not as bad as my husband, but after all what do you expect me to say? With his friends I bet he's different, then all of a sudden they're warm, then they become warm, because their friends, the men especially, make them happy, let's face it, not us, and not their kids. Don't look at me like that, you don't scare me. I changed your diapers. He looks at his mother and his wife with that face. *Che faccia brutta!* The Lentricchia men, they're all the same, believe me, except for one of my brother-in-laws who went to the other extreme. At least our husbands didn't do that, but maybe they should have, maybe they did that, too. Because let's face it, sex is another joke. What do you want me to say? *Why* are they like that around us? You went to college, you tell me. To be honest, I don't think even they know, and I don't care anymore, because in their own homes they don't want involvement, they go inside themselves. What are they doing in there? If they didn't want involvement, who told them to get married in the first place, if they didn't want involvement. What I want to know is how long are you going to kid yourself? If you have the answer, don't think I want to hear it, because I don't want to hear it, but if you have to, you can tell me."

I can't remember the words, I can't remember the context, maybe there wasn't one, because she doesn't need a context, but that's how I remember it now, five or six years later, my father in another room watching TV, my mother right in front of us, and I don't have to remind you who "us" is. She probably had a context; I just couldn't see it.

It should be mentioned that my mother is prone to opera. She talks in arias. Any and all disturbances presage apocalypse. Her enemies ought to croak, the bastards. All wounds are fatal, and anything can cause a wound, even nothing can cause a wound. It should also be mentioned that I've heard it said that I'm nothing like my father, who I'm not saying is what my mother says he is. According to him, I'm very like my mother. We're the same. "What do you expect? He exaggerates. He exaggerates everything. He gets it from his mother. He gets excited, don't you, Frank?" Arias without discernible context; emotions for which I can find no matching circumstances. Apocalypse twice a week. Wounds that cannot be healed, not even by affection. Affection, in fact, makes them much worse, opens them right up again.

About a year ago, in New York, an editor at a major publishing house said to me that I ought, up front, tell my readers who I am. Otherwise readers would have to crawl inside my head. She said "crawl inside." She felt that in order to understand the chunk she had just read, she would need to crawl inside my head, in order to find out who I am. When she told me that, I felt a strong urge to find out who she was. I wanted to open up her head. I should have said, "If I knew who the fuck I was, do you think I'd be writing this?" Or I should have said, "If I knew what the fuck I was doing, do you think I'd be writing this?" I was about to revise out "fuck," but if I did you might think that I was talking meta-phorically when I said I wanted to open up her head. In order to see what was under the skull, what was actually in there.

I was talking to the New York editor in my favorite Italian pastry shop, way over on the East Side, near the East Village, a place I liked to frequent because any time I went in there I saw an elegantly dressed elderly man, utterly mani-cured, a shave every four hours, a haircut every five days, who would occasionally walk outside to talk to youngish guys built like bulls in flowered shirts, with envelopes in their hands who kissed him on the cheek when they left. It was a movie, post-*Godfather*. They knew they were in a movie; they were enjoying themselves in the movie.

The elegantly dressed elderly man scared me. I had to look at him out of the corner of my eye, which I became very good at, because I didn't want to be in his movie in the wrong role. I've never seen a face that brutal when he thought no one was looking at the face. It was the best brutal face I'd ever seen. I liked to look at it. Maybe a plastic surgeon could give me a duplicate. They say anything can be arranged in New York.

It would have been nice to call him over, to introduce

him to the New York editor at a major house. Then I could have said, "Now say the words 'crawl inside your head' to this man." If only she could have coffee with this man every day, if only she could, she would become more sensitive in her relations with writers, she would become a good woman. Because if she didn't, with his demitasse spoon, and his little pinky sticking way out, he'd eat what was under her skull. I don't like questions about who I am or what I'm doing. If you wish to know who I am, ask my parents; they know. Or my friends, with whom it is said I'm different.

I'll tell you what I like about writing. When I'm doing it, there's only the doing, the movement of my pen across the paper, the shaping of rhythms as I go, myself the rhythm, the surprises that jump up out of the words, from heaven, and I am doing this, and I *am* this doing, there is no other "I am" except for this doing across the paper, and I never existed except in this doing.

I'll tell you what I hate about writing. Finishing it. It comes to an end. You can't come forever. When I'm finished, I can't remember what it was like inside the doing. I can't remember. When I'm not writing, I want to become the man with the brutal face.

A sentence, a sentence, my family for a sentence.

This time it's only a few months back that I'm trying to remember, so I'm fairly confident about the words. A telephone call to my parents, for the purpose of conducting research on a word famous in second-generation Italian-American households, who get it from the first generation, and then pass it on to the third, where I am, dead end of tradition. Forget the fourth, where my kids are. I was writing about this word. Once I heard this word spoken by Robert De Niro in Martin Scorsese's *Mean Streets* (I like to write out those names) and felt secretly addressed, even thrilled, a member of a community. Its pronunciation varied startlingly in my family, according to affective context: *c*'s become *g*'s; final vowels could disappear. It all depended. The word was deeply rooted, yet flexible. It gave what was needed. A genial word, from the unprinted lexicon of Italian-American. I pose the question of its meaning to my mother, who says immediately, "Pecker, your pecker." She's totally confident, so I don't mention that the interesting word takes the feminine definite article, because some part of me, maybe most of me, wants her to be right, with the feminine definite article, yes. My father only says, "Ann." That's all, you can hear him. My mother is not intimidated. She comes back: "I know that word." My father: "It's the woman's, *he* knows it's the woman's." He's totally confident. He tells her that I'm kidding around. He knows that, if asked, which I wasn't (because they don't do that), I'd side with him. After such phone calls, what knowledge?

I am an Italian-American, one of whose favorite words bears his grandparents, his parents, his neighborhood, his favorite movie director, but not his children, not his colleagues, not where he lives now, and not most of his friends. I'm not telling you that I'm alienated from my ethnic background.

I'm not alienated from it, and I'm not unalienated from it. It's an issue that doesn't much preoccupy me anymore.

This word dancing in my head cannot tell the difference between the man's and the woman's. The New York editor, who is an Italian-American, thinks it important to tell you that I'm an Italian-American. Are you glad to know that? Am I becoming clearer to you by the sentence? I know a word that means the man's and the woman's. Do you want to know my secret word? Shall we play with it together? You starting to crawl in?

I have a friend who lives in a good place, in South Carolina. His name is Leonard Cunningham. Leonard once said to me, in full knowledge that I am a married man: "You still a grumpy old bachelor?" One time I called the place where Leonard lives. The person at the other end, who was not Leonard, said something that I must have misheard, because I replied, "Am I Father Aelred?" I must have misheard. The person best in a position to know reminds me of a nightmare that I can't remember, king of the roof-rattlers, a full-throated screamer. It seems that I looked into my wallet for my driver's license, found it, it was mine all right, definitely mine, but it bore someone else's name and picture. It was definitely mine all right. Feel free, don't worry about it. Crawl in.

I said nothing when the New York editor said that I ought to tell my reader that I'm a literary scholar, a literary theorist, a professor of English, a critic, and I was rendered speechless when she whipped out a copy of the paperback edition of one of my books—bent and underlined—and quoted some sentences about my favorite philosopher, William James, which I didn't remember writing, then offered a commentary on those sentences (critic of a critic of a philosopher), which I couldn't understand, sipping my decaf cappuccino, then declared that *that* very passage, and others like it in my critical books, would help my readers to understand who I am. Tell them you're a literary critic.

At which point, in a tone as dead flat as I could manage, I should have said, "I've concluded, after much consultation with experts in the field, and much reflection, that, in spite of all the obvious resemblances, I'm nothing at all like T. S. Eliot." That's what I should have told the New York editor when we were sitting there in that pastry shop way down on First Avenue. "For example," I should have said, "what are the chances that Eliot ever ate" *(academic, very dry, hands about the coffee cup)* "three cannoli in one sitting, even as I do now?" I can tell she needs to think I'm funny, rather than something else. She'd prefer not to think of me and something else. I'd prefer that she think of me and something else. I say, "You think I'm funny? What's so funny? You want to be edited?" She is trying to smile, but she cannot do it. I'm winning. At which point I call over the wonderful brutal face and say *(leaning in, with concern),* "Which one of us would you prefer to ride home with on the deserted subway at 1:00 A.M., to the end of the line in Brooklyn, just one of us and you in the car? Which one? Be careful, don't answer too fast, and don't say both because we're not kinky. Don't even suggest kinky.

You got a gun? Which one? Choose, I'll count to five, then I'll tell him" *(broad winning grin)* "to do that thing with his demitasse spoon, which I imagined eight minutes ago, which I haven't told you about, because I want you to be surprised and tickled pink. You want to taste my cannoli? I'm Al Pacino in *Godfather II.* Who are you? All work and no play makes Frank a dull boy. Name that movie with Jack Nicholson!"

I teach English in a distinguished university. In my distinguished department, which is like all English departments I have known or heard about, we have virtually nothing in common, not even literature.

For the last two years I've been writing about T. S. Eliot, I'd better say trying to write about him. All work and no play. He is a fascination and a crisis. Honey, I'm home. The job of the literary critic is to explain, whatever else he may do, but Eliot's poetry is beyond explanation, though it has been explained *ad nauseam.* I get nauseous. His poetry, and I say this with total admiration, is unreasonable. Not unreasonably difficult, just unreasonable, which is why I find it fascinating. I'm also drawn to his explanations of the writing process. He means the process of writing a poem. I mean the process of writing anything, including a letter, or this, maybe especially this. What is this? I hate that question. Make me happy and hate it too, hate it too.

Eliot is responding to a German writer, Gottfried Benn, Eliot is always responding to some other writer, building, ripping off, making something new. Theft and the individual talent. Eliot says that writing begins with an "obscure impulse" (in other words, you don't know what you're doing). Or, he says, you're haunted by a demon "with no face, no name, nothing" (in other words, you don't know who you are, you don't have a face). Benn says, says Eliot, that we start with an "inert embryo," a "creative germ." Plus the language. "He has something germinating in him for which he must find words, but he cannot know what words he wants until he has found the words." When you have found the right words (which you can't know are right in advance) then the thing for which the words have to be found disappears. You have a poem. Writing is a journey in and through language; writing is discovery. That's Benn. Here's Eliot's twist: the writer "is oppressed by a burden which he must bring to birth in order to obtain relief." Eventually, the writer gains "relief from acute discomfort" (sounds like an ad for something) and experiences "a moment of exhaustion, of appeasement, of absolution, and of something very near annihilation, which is in itself indescribable." Benn never mentioned acute discomfort; Benn maybe likes the process. Eliot feels labor pains, or maybe a sharp gas pain in the lower intestinal tract. The pain gives no pleasure. What gives pleasure is the end, when relief is obtained, and the poem is fully born. The last *t* has been crossed, *then* Eliot is satisfied.

Coleridge is better than either Benn or Eliot on the writing process. He says readers "should be carried forward, not merely or chiefly by the mechanical impulse of curiosity, or by a restless desire to arrive at the final solution" (we know who you are, you're under arrest), "but by the pleasurable activity of mind excited by the attractions of the journey itself." He's talking about readers who almost don't exist, who don't ask questions that make me unhappy, who do not seek the final solution. No reader could possibly experience what Coleridge wants readers to experience unless (Coleridge is not talking now, it's me) there were writers who wanted to feel the same thing, "the pleasurable activity of the mind excited by the attractions of the journey itself." The meandering adventure through language (writing as drafting as revising as improvising), not the thing at the end but the unfolding process itself, the journey, the ride, every step of the way, never sure what's unfolding, never caring that much, happy to go off the track, screw the track. Outside the process, the demon has no name. The process names the demon and you are the demon, the demon *in* and *of* and *as* the process, and you like the demon. For once, you like yourself. The annihilation you experience is indescribably good, because it is the death of everything you were outside the process. The opaque burdens of your self-consciousness are lifted. When the process ends, you go back—the opacity, the weight, the stasis, and other things best not to mention, that's what you are. There you are, on the track.

When I'm doing this, whatever "this" is, and that's not my problem, that's your problem, if you want that problem, which you don't have to have because nobody is holding a gun to your head and demanding that you tell us what this is, when I'm doing this, I like taking walks, driving, riding in airplanes (I have an extra ticket, you want it free?), sitting in the waiting lounge, doing it there in public, when will my flight board? I can't wait. Motion like the motion of my pen. I can write in airplanes now. I become a dangerous driver, things come into my head when I drive and walk, writing as motion sickness, I better walk more. I *am* writing; *l'écriture, c'est moi.*

In a letter—on this one he didn't go public—Eliot had something to say about bad writing. Bad writing is writing that repeats what you've already written. To avoid it, you must "defecate" the self that produced it, if it is possible (which it isn't) to say a "self" produces the kind of writing that Eliot has in mind. Defecate the self *of* that writing, that's better, my graduate students might like that, or run the risk of writing feces. To avoid it, void it. Birth and defecation, labor pains and gas pains, life and crap. Does Eliot know the difference? Does anybody? Flesh of my flesh, shit of my shit. Shit of my death. I'm a literary critic.

It was in the place where Leonard lives that I first read these lines from Psalm 144:

> *No ruined wall, no exile,*
> *No sound of weeping in our streets.*

"Flesh of my flesh": Eliot's poem, his metaphorical child. I have two children, not metaphorical. We, I risk speaking for the three of us (I mean the two kids and me, Eliot has no part in this), we feel unrelieved, unappeased, not absolved, annihilated in quite specific ways, the details of which I'm never going to tell you. We are certainly exhausted. "Annihilated" is heavy, but I'm using it anyway. Eliot used it, why can't I? I'm not giving you the details because this isn't *People* magazine. The domestic details are banal, anyway. They don't explain. The opium of the middle class. You already know the details. You know the soap opera, so don't ask.

One weekend, a long time ago, about fifteen years back, when they were about five and six and a half, they were visiting us. You know who "us" is and you know why they were "visiting." While she was cooking dinner (no, I won't tell you her name, you don't need to know that, either), we played a game involving the stairs to the second floor. Daddy, you stand at the bottom. Daughter Number 1 climbs to the third stair. Daddy says, Amy Amy Amy. She jumps into his arms. Daughter Number 2. Rachel Rachel Rachel. Jumps into his arms. Daddy, let's do it again. Lots of giggling. We do it for the fourth stair. We do the fifth. Giggling becoming intense, hysteria creeping in, the little bodies flying, love-missiles right on target. Daddy Daddy Daddy. Amy Amy Amy. Rachel Rachel Rachel. Crash. The sixth is painful, gravity is beginning to talk tough. Daddy was not ready. The kids want the seventh. Daddy braces, the seventh is accomplished. Higher! Let's go higher! We do the eighth, my God. We do the ninety-eighth; we do the four hundred and fifty-eighth stair. Flesh of my flesh. We open up each other's heads. "I'll get you through our kids, you son of a bitch." *I'll get the kids through you, you son of a bitch, I'll put the kids through you, you son of a bitch, I'll put the son of a bitch through the kids, you son of a bitch, I'll put the son of a bitch through the son of a bitch, with the full cooperation of the son of a bitch, you son of a bitch.* What do you expect? I'm middle-class. I like soap opera too.

We didn't have a name for the game we played. I think I was saving them. It was the game of I Saved the Kids. "He exaggerates. He exaggerates everything." Like my mother, I'm prone to it, prone to the real thing, where they go all the way, all the time the four hundred and fifty-eighth stair. The real thing is Italian opera. Can this shit live? Can this shit sing?

"You need to tell us where you're from."
"I'm one hundred percent from literature."
"No, seriously."
"Okay. I'm one hundred percent from the movies."

A conversation that never took place, with the New York editor or with anyone else. No real conversation about my first place. Good thing, it would have been too hard to explain in conversation, to say just what I mean. The first place, my so-called origins, the Hydrogen Bomb of explanation. Then everything becomes clear. Then everything becomes dead. In conversation with strangers I tend to be sloppy and anxious, sometimes with intimates, too, what an experience that is. Conversation is too hard. Better to write. Forget the telephone, forget talking altogether. Except after long, enforced absences, talking is overrated.

Yeats said that he was always discovering places where he wanted to spend his whole life. One of the places where I want to spend my whole life is in Yeats. Like Yeats, I don't know exactly where I'm supposed to be. Long after I left, long after it seemed to have drifted out of my mind for good, Yeats helped me to recover my first place, my grandfather's house on 1303 Mary Street, Utica, New York, where we lived on the second floor until I was a senior in college. But "recover" is misleading, suggesting I got something back that I used to possess. I used to sleep and eat there, but I never possessed it, it never possessed me (that's better), I never actually lived there until I imagined myself all the way back through the medium of some of Yeats's poems about the great country houses of Ireland, specifically Lady Gregory's, Augusta Gregory's (she had just the right first name), in the west of Ireland, Coole Park, where Yeats was taken in every summer, nurtured and sustained and respected for who he was, a writer. Coole Park was the place where he wrote well and about which, much later, he would write better than well, he would write magnificently, out of his memory of loving sustenance and respect, poems about the place itself, writing when he had a bitter hunch, and he was right, that the place would be leveled, imagining its and his own not being there, and the vines and the saplings winning, forcing themselves up through the broken stone, the rubble. He wrote magnificently because he was haunted.

Absurd to think of my grandfather's house—my mother's father's house—and Coole Park in tandem, neck and neck in my imagination, absurd to say that I possessed it as if for the first time, not as if but actually, reading poems about an aristocratic mansion, where my grandfather would have been employed to "shovel shit," which is what he would say whenever I asked him to tell me what he did in the old country, when he was young. He shoveled it for *il padrone,* the landlord, which he said in his dialect: *u padron.* He was speaking literally, and he said *u padron* with a tone perfectly mixed with resentment, awe, and desire.

He, my mother's father, Tomaso was his name, could have been one of Lady Gregory's writers, because he was the best storyteller I ever heard. He had an endless supply featuring surprising savage ironies, beautiful twists of revenge, twists of revenge are always beautiful, those stories were wonderful because people got what they had coming to them, the bastards. And the supply must have been endless because he told them every night and he never repeated himself except by special request. I never heard of any of them before or since. I believe he made them up, I hope he did, as we sat there around the kitchen table, spurring him on just by showing him how happy we were because he was telling us stories. He could see we hung on his words and gestures. We were helping him to make them up, that's what we were doing, though nobody could have known that, much less said it. We were imagining together, that's what I believe. Of course, we could never have done what he did, and he was not born to listen to stories.

After supper, after the espresso, the anisette, and the Stella d'Oro cookies, and several of us there waiting for him to start, he would turn it on without warning. We would sometimes ask for repetitions, a story he told last month, and he would oblige, but on occasion he would balk (briefly) and display a flare of irritation (briefly), when my father or I (the main requesters) would ask for a certain story too soon, like four days later (at which point we became the main aggravations). He would look at us, say oh my Jesus Christ, then deliver it as if for the first time, as if for a virgin audience, as if he himself had heard it for the first time six minutes ago, he himself laughing hard in the funny moments. Later, my father and I would say some of the key lines and words to each other, going back upstairs, as if we never heard them before, doing some of his gestures, going to bed with his voice jumping in our heads. If I could tell you how good he was, I mean so that you knew the way we knew, you'd miss him even though you never experienced him in the flesh.

One night, we got out of hand, my father and I. We asked for the one we liked best too soon, we asked the night after he told it, and then we became worse than an aggravation. Tomaso said nothing. He just got up, walked over to the refrigerator, looked in for about twelve seconds (which in a situation like that you can imagine what it felt like), took nothing out, even though he must have needed something bad, shut the door, came back to the table, then told it ferociously. His fury made it new. When he was finished, he got up and went to bed. It was barely dusk. I wish that I could remember that one, I'd tell it to you right now. But maybe that's what you get for abusing the storyteller, you lose your memory of the story. He withdrew that night, and now the story is withdrawn forever.

His sons and sons-in-law referred to him openly as the King of Mary Street, without irony, with pride. His depressions were rare but deep, and if he happened to be suffering one when they addressed him as the King of Mary Street, he'd come back with, I am the King of Pig Street. Or he'd say, the King of the Pricks, I am the Prick of Mary Street, I am the King of the Pigs. I wonder if Lady Gregory ever thought of herself as the Cunt of Coole Park? You can't tell about those aristocrats. Like artists and peasants like Tomaso, they're capable of anything. They tend not to give a damn what people think.

One of my father's brothers came up with the one he liked best. The King of the Mushrooms (always with the definite articles), not because of the quantities he could put away, but because of the huge Santa Claus sacks full he would bring home every weekend, every autumn—he knew where they were in the damp and shady secret places in the hills around Utica, to which he'd walk, ten, twelve miles round-trip every weekend (one time I heard twenty-two miles), usually on a Sunday morning when Natalina, his wife, was at church. Even into his late sixties. At today's prices who knows the value. Maybe 300 pounds per autumn. Which my grandmother would put up, and her daughters and daughters-in-law would put up, a year's worth for the family, free.

On Thanksgiving he took everybody, about forty people, to an "American" restaurant, because if I want Italian food I'll stay home. But on most major holidays, we all ate at his table, two or three shifts, too many courses, the men falling asleep right there during coffee. I never saw one of the women fall asleep.

I never saw him reading. The only thing he ever wrote were the bills, with curses against the Blessed Virgin Mary. Lady Gregory listened to Irish peasants, then wrote it all down (who knows what she changed) and made books out of illiterate genius. If he had had a Lady Gregory, then you'd know. He was a Lady Gregory and he needed a Lady Gregory, but he couldn't be his own Lady Gregory.

I liked the wide black belt he wore with the huge

buckle, I have one just like it, and I like to remember the way his belly, emphasized by the belt, spilled over it. My belly's starting to do the same thing, but he never did what I do. He never held it in; he just let it spill over; he let it cascade. If you could have asked him why he didn't hold it in (the question was culturally inconceivable), he'd reply in one of his favorite idioms. The crude English equivalent is: "Because I don't give a fuck." The crude Italian says: "Because it doesn't fuck me."

Without fail, every third summer, the sons and the sons-in-law painted his house. And every other summer, it bore fruit, that audacious thing he cultivated, that cherry tree—he and the sons and the sons-in-law mounting the longest extension ladder he could buy. He made that thing go beyond itself, "in nature's spite" (Yeats's phrase for a work of art, what we rear "in nature's spite"). He definitely reared that tree. It was thirty-five feet high when it was supposed to be only eighteen, and however wide a thirty-five-foot cherry tree would have to be, that's how wide it was. That cherry tree got too big and too old, so he reared it more, he got up under its ass with two-by-fours, bracing the big limbs that couldn't take it anymore. Then he made those long black belts, gargantuan versions of the one he wore around his waist, he must have bred those tree belts, he must have pulled those tree belts right out of his own belt, and he stopped that tree from doing what it wanted to do, but it started to do it anyway, and the sap ran out of the gashes, so he poured stuff into the gashes that looked like actual concrete, which I think it was, and he stopped the gashes from getting worse, but later they got worse anyway.

And every other summer they climbed it, I was too young to be trusted on the extension ladder, with a great basket and a little hook attached to the great basket's handle, for the rungs, so you wouldn't have to hold the basket once you got up into it, and with a long stick, hooked at the end, it looked like a cane for a giant—I think he made it from an old cane of his, which he grafted an extension onto, which grew one-sixteenth of an inch every other summer—that cane was so the men could reach way out where no ladder could go, where only the goddamn robins could (and did) go, and where (naturally, damn the Virgin Mary) the best cherries were, but that cane at the end of a grown man's arm got out there all right and they pulled in those cherries in robins' spite, fuck those robins, because that's what Yeats was trying to put across, and they pulled in enough cherries for an army. And so they had to put them up, of course, Natalina, and the daughters, and the daughters-in-law.

It was family socialism, the men risking their necks, you could hardly see them up in there, up against that tree that sprawled way over into Louie Spina's yard, who was welcome to pick everything on his side, but he always asked before he did it, even though he knew the answer, and the women getting scalded in the kitchen, you think it didn't happen?, it happened, more than once, and risking their sanity doing that tedious repetitive shit they have to do on an assembly line, without the adventure of the tree, being up in there when the tree belts might go at any minute, the wisecracks going back and forth between the guys on the ground and the guy in the tree. I heard some odd talk in the kitchen, those women let go because I was too young to be harmful, and I saw sullenness in that kitchen, like a pure thing. Those women were anxious to tear into somebody. I think they had a critique of socialism.

He commanded loyalty and energy, I don't know how. Nobody was afraid of him because there wasn't any big inheritance awaiting the best ass-kisser. Some ass-kissing, naturally, went on, because one or two thought there was a pile stashed away, but those one or two kissed his ass in vain. His personality was on the sweet side, and he was known to cry. Maybe it was the fig tree. If you can believe a fig tree at that latitude, which you have to because I'm telling you it was there, but I can't go into all that he did to rear it, it would take too long, and I haven't even gotten to the other grandfather yet, you know, the one who was so cold you don't even know what I mean by cold. The grandfather who produced the son who produced me. The genealogy of ice, according to the leading soprano. ("He gets excited. He thinks he's the leading tenor, don't you, Frank?") Maybe it was the combination of the storytelling, the mushroom mountains he brought home, and the fig tree. Thomas the August. All I'll tell you is that if that cherry tree wanted to put out cherries the size of golf balls, then he gave that fig tree major hubris. There were maybe only seven figs per summer, but they pumped themselves up to the pear level, it's true. Maybe if your grandfather or your father or your father-in-law could do what he did for cherries and figs, you'd want to work for Tomaso, you might not be able to keep yourself from throwing in with him, no matter how irritated you might get sometimes, which you would definitely get because he couldn't or wouldn't drive, and you'd have to pull driving duty once a month, and drag your wife with you against her will, and your kids losing it in the backseat, once a month, on a Sunday, when maybe you were fed up with the extended family routine, who could blame you if you were fed up once a month?, but just on that day when you were completely fed up you'd have to pull driving duty, take him up to his camp on Oneida Lake, "to the beach," *u beach.*

He had two camps at Sylvan Beach, next to each other, and the big one, the size of a small hotel, burned to the ground and almost got the other one, too. They said "some bum" did it in the winter, but the crime was never solved, and he went into a depression almost as long as the one he went into after the near-lethal heart attack, a depression, according to my father, that lasted a year, he was mourning for his own death, but it turned out he outlived death by twenty-four years, no talking except for yes and no and an occasional because it doesn't fuck me. What I'm saying is that if this man is in your family, and I didn't screw up the tense just then, if this man is in your family, you want to be on his side, don't tell me you wouldn't. You wouldn't burn the camp. You wouldn't do something to the cherry tree in the middle of the night. No Italian would do a thing like that. Americans do that.

I know what you're thinking. You're thinking, he's making a story out of that grandfather of his and that cherry tree. (I cannot tell a lie.) You just don't know my concept of truth, my conception (that's better), and I don't think you ought to worry about it either, which I'm not saying you're doing. Those kinds of worries are not worth it. The distinction between truth and fiction, that one gets tougher and tougher for me to get. I'm going to stop trying to get it, because it doesn't fuck me.

The first place, 1303 Mary Street, technically doesn't qualify because the first four or five years of my life were spent a few doors east, up the block. East was always "up"; west was always "down," because it led to downtown Utica. I begin with the basic fact, that the first place wasn't the first place (Yeats wasn't born in Coole Park either); I add to that another fact, that the so-called first place dropped out until I reread Yeats two years ago, just before traveling to Ireland, as I was starting this book, which I didn't know I was starting; then I add an assertion, which I want you to believe, though you might not: that I wouldn't go back, even if I could (and I can) because I don't feel any return-pain (no nostalgia, *that* you don't believe), because what I want from the first place I draw on freely. No, better to say it draws on me, like sucking, even now, sitting here writing. Yeats taught me that the first place was about writing. (No, not "about," "about" should be revised out.) Small second-floor spaces, first on Mary Street in the late forties and through the fifties, now here in Hillsborough, North Carolina, and a relationship to something made possible by those spaces. I am here in the first place.

"A relationship to something": I'm not sure of the name. Not a relationship *to,* no, as if the "something" were a person or geographical point. The relationship *is* the something, and the place is itself the relationship. The place is me-in-the-place, so if I'm not there, then the place is no longer the place, and I am no longer me. If you lose the first place, which almost everybody does, it's not a tragedy. The story still might turn out well.

So I am going to be drawn by these lines in Yeats, drained almost dry:

> *O may she live like some green laurel*
> *Rooted in one dear perpetual place.*

Yeats, praying for his newborn daughter, and creating unnecessary pain for himself, and for me, by writing "perpetual." He should have forgotten "perpetual," he should have revised it out, because she's going to be rooted in a dear perpetual place that she'll lose, then, with luck (I have no idea how), she'll find a new perpetual place.

The "something" comes closer when I read this, concerning the pleasures of an ancestral house:

> *The pacing to and fro on polished floors*
> *Amid great chambers and long galleries, lined*
> *With famous portraits of our ancestors; . . .*

Tomaso had one in his dining room, a picture of his mother and father, which now hangs in mine, a portrait famous only in my family, and now among some few of my friends. Yeats was describing the house of a rich man. But it's not the things of the house, it's never the things, no matter how lovely the things, because there are always lovelier. It's the looking and the pacing to and fro. My floors are polished, and I pace the house between sentences, on my polished floors, looking for sentences, they're mine now, these polished floors. Yeats's

poetic place, Tomaso's, where I am now, houses that look
like they've been meditated upon, they have that kind of
look, the look is there in the floors, and in the narrow stairs to
the second floor, this is a house, this is, this is what truly is,
and it looks like it has been looked at, this house of mine, with
a yearning (Yeats gives me these words, they are his gift) with
a yearning so great that the yearning drowns in its own excess:

> *Beloved books that famous hands have bound,*
> *Old marble heads, old pictures everywhere;*
> *Great rooms where travelled men and children found*
> *Content or joy; . . .*

He was there, at Coole Park, to write, that was his role, and
to stroll magnificent grounds, and to approach the small lake
at Coole, when the sun flares cruelly off the waters, and to
gaze as if with lidless eyes into the glare as they climb the
air, the swans mounting invisible through the sun-flare, just
for him, honored guest of gazing. My role—I was the
fussed-over grandson (a redundancy)—mine was to study,
not to work like the men and the women, and to be sustained at 1303 Mary Street, for the leisure of my intellect,
for my long apprenticeship in pure gazing. I, too, was an
honored guest ("He gets good marks, he's smart in
school").

When I was there, Tomaso was my Lady Gregory, the
house on Mary Street my Coole Park. I was Tomaso's ap-
prentice writer. He was the master, the writer who couldn't
write, the talking writer. These lines from "Coole Park,
1929" suck me, too, deep into their vision:

> *They came like swallows and like swallows went,*
> *And yet a woman's powerful character*
> *Could keep a swallow to its first intent;*
> *And half a dozen in formation there,*
> *That seemed to whirl upon a compass-point, . . .*

Hard not to notice, it's a small poem, Yeats's saying "there" five times, a strategic incantation, bringing "there" here, making it thingy, and you stand in it, on it, take your stand there.

And because he, Tomaso, was "there," his powerful character holding us all in formation, I could stand there on the small second-floor back porch, a space five by five, the cherry tree at my right, at the twenty-foot level, at the level of the tips where only the robins and the giant cane could go, and the fig tree tucked in against the garage, at the back of the yard, the tomato plants next door on my left, looked at from above, and my grandfather's garden totally shaded by the cherry tree (he made it grow in sun's spite), and Louie Spina in his yard on my right, Louie invisible through the cherry tree, moving heavily about, who laid brick with arms like your thighs, thighs like your boy's waist, and me standing in the dusk after supper, I'd walk out there, drawn, belly full, no one moving now down there in the yards, legs becoming stone, it will take serious effort to leave (turn body, pick up feet), and the yard is quiet, leaning into the railing, automatic hands picking off the flaking paint (it's *next* summer the men must do that), the yard is calm, and the looker looks into quiet and calm more juicy than those huge cherries just hanging there, becomes part of another life, not his, he just drops into it, he goes in, sucked all the way into the juicy quiet and calm, full in his belly, twelve years old, just gazing there.

Okay, the other grandfather, my father's father. If I write down his first name, I'll secure a cheap irony, not to mention the melodrama of shocking coincidence. In melodrama, as in Italian opera, the writer makes deplorably excessive appeals to the emotions of the audience, he'll do anything, like tell you that the name of his father's father, the Patriarch of Ice, the Origin of Ice, is Augusto. Cheap.

It was said he baby-sat me in the early forties. Then, still in the early forties, he and my grandmother, Paolina, moved to Miami because the rich people, for whom he had strong left-wing contempt, like to go there in the winter, and they know the good places, and because he thought it would ease his arthritis, which it didn't. After they moved, I saw him a few times in the summer, when they came to visit, he always sending Paolina ahead, then coming himself two weeks later, and I saw him on two visits that I made to Florida. When he died in 1980, the last of the grandparents to go (I was forty then), his oldest daughter sent me a surprise, several volumes of poetry and notebooks, he had been writing all those years, teaching himself Dante, the poems all written in a consistently elegant hand, in large five-by-eight diary books, the volumes numbered, his picture the frontispiece of volume one, the entire set entitled *Le Memorie di Augusto Lentricchia*. Family pieces (picnics, birthdays, births, deaths, the day Paolina was breaking a box in the kitchen for firewood and the splinter by intention flew into her eye, destroying her sight in that eye);

public events (strikes, Sacco and Vanzetti, Hoover, the death of Lenin, especially strikes, laborers in hell); poems to Paolina. From denunciatory satire, to domestic commemorations, to the romantic lyric, 1,200 pages of work, spanning the years between 1920 and his death.

His sons and daughters knew he was writing all those years, but they never thought it important to mention this to me, the professor of English, of whom they were very proud, don't get me wrong. Every year he'd mail me a serious book: Michelangelo, Einstein, Thomas Paine, Walt Whitman. He was following my educational progress with pleasure, he said so in his letters. He wrote a poem about his grandson in graduate school at Duke University, but he never showed it to me. They said he was a champion baby-sitter, that's the phrase they used, they always said that. After his death, I quizzed his oldest daughter about it: "Because you would go to bed early, and you were a quiet kid, anyway. The grown-ups would go out and he'd take care of you so he wouldn't have to go out, so he could stay home and write, which he loved." I don't know why he took those thirty-hour train rides from Miami to Utica by himself. I'm guessing he wanted the private time for his writing. Not to mention the two weeks before, all by himself, which must have been wonderful.

He was a neat and a disciplined man. He ironed his own clothes, which always looked as if they'd been laundered and pressed only an hour ago. Calisthenics every morning. Mostly silent at the dinner table. His crew-cut silver hair looked like it was trimmed every five days, and no matter how hot and humid the day, he looked cool and contemplative. Perfect flat belly. When he spoke it was always like he was forcing the voice to come out; soft and cracked, broken up; the voice didn't want to speak; it wasn't used to it; the voice didn't want to go public. He was polite, even courtly in manner, especially with Paolina, but he wasn't interested in conversation. He was interested in reading and writing, and his kids weren't, and when he baby-sat me in the early forties we were a good team. The Patriarch of Ice and Baby Ice. Learning the ropes.

Of course, I've heard some stories, but I'll never tell them. First of all, I consider the sources: nonwriters. Second, I don't care. So what that he did a few things? Of course, my mother wasn't talking about a few things he did, she was talking about the tone of his presence, the quality of being, his and hers, when she had to be in the same room with the man. Am I supposed to believe that Pacino learned how to do *Godfather II* from him? Revenge is a meal best taken cold. Applies inside the family, too. She comes back to see the kids after the separation, you remember, Diane Keaton, who when she told him she was leaving him, when she was leaving him, remember?, he says "I'll change," with that dead look on his face. How come Al didn't say, Diane, you change, because I'm not changing. And so she's standing there, just outside the threshold of the house in Vegas, saying good-bye to the kids, when he comes into view from another room, tanned and terrific looking, Al never looked better, and with the best pitiless look I've ever seen on that face of his that you can't take your eyes off of, and the look is delightful. (I must contact a very good plastic surgeon.) And he says nothing. Diane says, Hello, Michael. Al says nothing. He just closes the door in her face like death. Al didn't change. Later, in *Godfather III,* we see what happens. Diane changed. You changed, Diane, do you feel better now? Let them change, because we're not.

I don't want to contradict my mother, not because she's my mother, and there's nobody I'd rather sit and listen to, but because I believe that her feelings had grounds. All I'm saying is that I don't care. And I'm saying that I consider the source: a nonwriter, by which I don't mean bad. I mean nonwriter. My theory, which I haven't told my mother yet, is that her smoking wasn't the thing. He was aggravated because he couldn't get back to the writing, or because he was blocked, or because he was writing well and wanted to get back to it, or because he worked on the kitchen table, he had no choice, and how was he supposed to write with that loud mob (the family) in the house? The louder the mob the more he concentrated on that phrase in his head that he was going to write down tomorrow. That's just a theory of mine. Did he find intimacy on a daily basis too much work? The phrase he honed in his head, that was the thing, he liked that phrase.

Pacino and Paolina used to take walks every evening after supper, and they never invited anyone to go with them. What does that mean? I can believe that his family didn't have access, that they felt shut out, because he floated inside his own mind too much, because he wasn't one of those who constantly exude sympathy. You're there and he isn't, and you take it personally. They would think him cold. What else could they do? Assume that he was trying to be himself?

Every afternoon, Monday through Friday, she'd call him (I saw this in Florida) at 4:00 P.M., from the screened-in front porch where he sat with a book. So that they could watch a soap opera together. *The Edge of Night.* "Augu, *Edge' a Night.*" I'm not telling you they were lovers until the day she went into her final coma. He ignored something in her will, according to one of his sons. I have no idea about the nature of their relationship. Did he show her the poems, the ones about herself that she couldn't read? Did he read them to her? What if he didn't? What would that prove? The fact that a man who likes to write writes a tender poem to a woman doesn't necessarily mean what it is supposed to mean. Maybe it means that he enjoyed writing the poem, period.

Paolina was the shyest person I've ever known, but when she said, "Augu, *Edge' a Night,*" and he didn't hear because he was lost in that book of his on the screened-in porch, she said it again in a surprising tone. He came with a very small grin. He sat down; no talking; they watched the television intensely; no discussion during the commercials. After the episode was concluded, there was talk about plot details, getting it straight, preparing for tomorrow's intensity.

It's possible that marriage and kids were a mistake. It's possible he knew that. It's possible he was, at times, seething underneath because he knew that he shouldn't have gotten married, et cetera, because he did some things that could have been a lot worse, and he knew they could have, but he held back and had waking visions of himself doing the unspeakable, going way over the edge, getting himself onto the front page of the newspaper. It's possible. I have no knowledge of his nightmares; I'm only imagining.

• • •

Now I shall write out my desire for a dead man. This is what I want. That he, Augusto, could have been his, Tomaso's, Yeats. That in the warm months a little writing table would be placed for him out there on the second-floor back porch. That he would sleep out there when he wished. That in cold weather he be permitted into the finished part of the cellar, where he'd find a full kitchen and be given a key to the special cellar within the cellar, under lock and key except to Tomaso, Natalina, and now Augusto, a key to the inner cellar, lined with what to my eyes and his look like bookcases, where he shall find space to place his few books and his manuscripts, in between the canned goods, the cherries and peaches and pears, the mushrooms and sausage and caponata, and the tomatoes and peppers and beets, and on the floor against the coolest wall, Tomaso's cool homemade wine, as cool as himself. And when he wanted something to sweeten the day, he would only have to speak his desire, and she would bring him one of her homemade cannoli, stuffed only upon the voicing of desire. A pallet would be fit into the inner cellar and he would sleep in there, but only in the cold months. Then one fine day at midmorning in midsummer he would look up from his writing table on the porch (this is what I most want for him) and know the quiet like the pen in his hand and legal pad beneath, part of the lines he writes when he likes the lines, part of what he most wants to be and, in that moment, is, sensing himself inside a relationship more primordial than what it holds in relation. Then he knows, and is, what Yeats said about Homer:

> . . . *Homer had not sung*
> *Had he not found it certain beyond dreams*
> *That out of life's own self-delight had sprung*
> *The abounding glittering jet; . . .*

Life's, not Augusto's, self-delight, I want him to be lost in that, life's self, which was the world of Tomaso, and then from Augusto would spring, as it had sprung from Homer, the abounding glittering jet, expression pouring forth, piling high upon itself, the lines he would most like, lines that were part of the quiet and the self-delight of which he himself was only part.

And let it be his death room, the second-floor back porch, let it be detached and boarded up, and let him be buried in it between the fig tree and the cherry tree, and upon the grave let there be placed a sprig of cherry, one fig, and, each day, one mushroom, one for every time he could press back, almost without knowing he was pressing back, almost without pain, his urges for marriage and fatherhood. Let it all be.

Augu, *Edge a Night.*

PART ONE

To the Monastery

May–September 1991

1

Prayer is pure and perfect, according to the authority of St. Anthony, when the contemplative no longer realizes that he is praying or indeed that he exists at all.   —THOMAS MERTON

Occasionally, on the campus of Duke University, where I teach, I run into Stanley Hauerwas, a man I am drawn to but hardly know. Stanley is a major force in theological ethics and the commander of the only unself-conscious foulmouth in the professoriate. I hear they complain about him at his home in the Divinity School. Stanley is lean and totally focused.

Why did he say, out of nowhere, that I should meet Mike Baxter, of all people? Maybe because I once told him that I was an ex-Catholic and considered myself a half-assed ascetic. Stanley would not have paid attention to "half-assed" and he probably thinks "ex-" can't go in front of "Catholic."

Mike Baxter is a Roman Catholic priest, studying under Stanley for his Ph.D. Stanley is not a Catholic.

I'd never had an interest in religion, especially the words that go with religion. Especially the word "God," which I wish people wouldn't use, even those who believe. Stanley believes. Stanley once told me that the point of his life was to worship "God." He doesn't speak in quotation marks. I believed him. Myself, I worship what they call "literature," another word that bothers me. I worship some of it. Most of it is like everything else.

I was surprised (still am) that I wasn't able to resist Stanley's suggestion, that I prolonged the accident of our encounter, and that I let myself give in, even though something in me was truly loathe to give in. Since there is always something in me truly loathe to give in, I am describing a banality, not a crisis. I told Stanley to tell Mike to call me. I couldn't manage it on my own, but of course I didn't admit that to Stanley. About ten days later I heard from Mike Baxter. We would go to dinner.

The first thing that hit me about Mike, startled me a little, was his eyes, but not because they're blue verging on gray. This man's eyes looked like those of a boxer who has just taken a crushing shot, flush on the jaw, and he's about to go, staring into the far distance, glassy. But at the time I didn't think, This guy's about to go. At the time I thought nothing. At the time I was a little scared by the look. The truth is, as soon as Stanley informed me of his existence, I wanted to talk to Mike Baxter. Understand, I had no desire to "meet" him; I was doing research on a touchy subject, maybe a touchy-feely subject. But I didn't tell Stanley that either, and the question was, how would I bring it up to Mike, a total stranger? I wonder what Stanley told him? Why was *he* supposing we were getting together? I'm betting Mike didn't bother to ask himself the question, and I'm betting that he, too, had a reason that had nothing to do with "meeting" me, which he would never tell me, even if I asked, and I never asked.

My reason was this: I wanted Mike's reaction to something that had been happening to me over the last two or three years. "Happening to me" is dull but correct. I told him that these—what?—had always had the same prelude: solitude, perfect quiet in the late morning, the end of a period of work on the writing of the day, an empty house with not even the two cats around, and me gazing aimlessly through the rear windows into the backyard, a dense enclosure of trees and bushes. I'm not sure "prelude" is the word. I'm not sure that I'm not talking about the thing itself. I wonder, at these moments, what I look like. A boxer who has just taken a crushing shot, flush on the jaw? Am I about to go, or have I just returned?

I wasn't seeking the considered judgment of a man of "God." Mike doesn't speak in quotation marks either. What I wanted from Mike was confirmation, I wanted him to supply the significance, to say *yes*. Naturally, I didn't tell him that. And I held back a crucial piece of information, another consistent motif in the prelude, if these were preludes. I never told him that these times occur only after the writing has gone well, in moments of unshakable satisfaction, when I neither regret the past nor strain to peer into the future—concerning writing or anything else. Never mind that the following morning, when I sit down with yesterday's pages, my satisfaction will be shook to death.

I know enough theology to know that hopelessness for the future is the technical definition of despair, the denial of God, the ground of suicide. What I was feeling in those moments was outside hope and its despair. I was inoculated against the past and the future, granted immunity from guilt and disappointment. I found myself floating in carelessness, the ground of nothing at all. I told Mike, mustering my best style of philosophic sophistication, that I wouldn't call what I was trying to tell him about "good," because I couldn't choose it. If the good is good then we must seek the good, else how can we be good? I declared it, triumphantly, beyond good and evil. Mike smiled a small smile.

Not even now can I read the smile. Mike doesn't give you those face contorters, the kind that lay us open to inspection. I had zapped him with a twinkling irony from a safe distance. I could do small smiles. If he were reminded, at that moment, that he was a graduate student and that I was not—he knew who I was all right—then good, we were even, because I knew who he was all right: a priest. What the hell was he giving me back? An ironic retort to my irony? These small smilers think they know our secrets. He was trying to drag me someplace, this punch-drunk man of God. He was trying to get me to say a particular word, and it wasn't "God" or "mysticism," but I prevailed. I didn't say it. Instead, I reached, I drew quickly: "pure consciousness," "sudden immediacies of light," "the landscape moved in closer, like a presence," "the quiet got bigger." I was phrasing; I repressed the subject at hand.

Mike was relaxed, talking easily. He wasn't phrasing, his eyes were looking maybe normal. He was smiling those small smiles. He had something on me, but he was probably okay. Then he fired the silver bullet. During dessert—no one has ever done in a dessert with more careful, unremitting attention—he mentioned that over spring break he had spent some time at a Trappist monastery. Mepkin Abbey, in South Carolina, a five-hour drive from Durham. What you see right away, he said, is that these people are happy. All you have to do is take one look at them and you know. It's obvious.

I recovered myself with a reference to Thomas Merton. Then Mike said a few things about Merton, but I remember only one—his opinion that the famous Merton autobiography, *The Seven Storey Mountain,* the international best-seller, translated into who knows how many languages, the book that brought many to the monasteries in the fifties and sixties, for retreats and forever, this book, Mike said, was, in his opinion, "a little pious."

I hadn't read a word of Merton: another part of the sixties that never happened for me. I didn't mention this to Mike. The only thing I knew about Merton was what everyone knew: that he gave up sex, drinking, and a promising literary career in order to enter Gethsemani Abbey, a Trappist monastery somewhere in Kentucky, back in the days when the rules were severe and you communicated largely through sign language. It turned out he had a major literary career anyway.

The next day I called Mike to tell him that I had made up my mind. What I said to him sounded to me, even then, in the grip of my enthusiasm, like bad writing. This is what I literally said to him: "As soon as you said that you went to the monastery, I knew I wanted to do that, all my life." I called a friend who I like to imagine has always lived in a Trappist monastery, a monk of writing. He said, "Take me with you." He's fifty-four. I called another friend—all his life, a monk of rock and roll. He said, "That's so brilliant, man." He's about to turn forty and I have been feeding him visions of the horror ever since he made it to thirty-nine. I'm fifty. About the happiness of those monks of God—it's obvious—I said nothing to Mike.

I walked past the security checkpoint and picked out a man in the small crowd waiting for arriving passengers. Long-sleeved black shirt, buttoned to the collar; gray pants, black shoes, and glasses; dramatic widow's peak, salt-and-pepper wavy hair, brushed back hard; cheekbones startling in their prominence. Older than me. Stern. Who else could it be? I was still maybe fifteen yards away. I darted a self-conscious glance to my left, De Niro–like, freeing myself for a split second, then back on him. He knew who I was. He said, "Frank," but the voice didn't match: too young, too easy, like a boy, not yet a teenager, asking if you (yourself not yet a teenager) could come out and play. They had sent Leonard Cunningham to the airport to get me.

In the van I came to the conclusion that I was being taken for someone else. Leonard Cunningham thought I was a lot younger; he thought I was a prospect who had come to look the place over. Leonard Cunningham was giving me his philosophy of entry, a warning. His views were strong, no doubt he had let the abbot himself know, more than once. Never mind that Mepkin Abbey had no novices, that it hadn't had any for some time, that the median age there is sixty-four. People weren't choosing the life and Mepkin Abbey was dying.

A man needs to have a sense of accomplishment before he comes, said Father Cunningham. Otherwise he leaves after a short while. I asked him what he meant by "a short while." He said five to ten years. I had to clear up the confusion; I was imagining myself inside his misconception, going all the way; I was terrorizing myself. So I revealed my occupation, my purposes, my age. "You carry it beautifully," he said. I took brief but major pleasure in the compliment, then concentrated, mercilessly, on the aggravating little pronoun. "You're looking at sixty-eight years of humanity," he said. He had been a monk for thirty-one.

About halfway there we stopped at a self-service gas station. A small man in a big, grimy American model of the seventies pulled around to another pump. The panic of imagining myself as Brother Frank, a monk at Mepkin Abbey, was being replaced by something else, a hundred times worse. I was grotesque, an alien on my own planet. The windows of the van were rolled up. What was a self-service gas station or a big grimy American model of the seventies? Things were falling away. Leonard Cunningham got back into the van and we drove on and I was asking him where he was from and he was saying "I'm a black man from Charleston." He's lighter than me. I made some guesses that I kept to myself. I was cold. Leonard Cunningham was beginning to look black and I didn't know where I was supposed to be.

A few weeks before I flew down to South Carolina, I bought several of Merton's books. I got through only the first twenty or so pages of *The Seven Storey Mountain*; the details of the secular life promised to be endless, the route to Gethsemani a boring prospect. I wanted the thing itself but was too conscientious to cut to the chase. Merton's contemplative books—Mike loaned me one the night we had dinner, making the extravagant claim that he "knew" I would like it—these books were short and lyrically knotty and uncluttered by mundane autobiography. I ate them up. Books about becoming empty; books about the struggle to defeat distraction; about letting go so that happiness in the form of God could enter and fill you up. One's "happiness" (a word worse than "God" or "literature") is always the lurking subject, if not at hand, then close at hand.

Merton was good at describing the agony in stony places but I suspect he held back on the lonely pleasures of his ravishment. I wondered about his constant return to the theme of community, the importance of the liturgy. In *The Rule of St. Benedict*, the law of monastic life for over a thousand years, it says that the punishment of a grave fault in a monk is exclusion from the common table. "No one shall speak or meet with him. He shall work alone. . . ." The punishment assumes the desirability of community and the pain of isolation. But didn't "monk" derive from a Greek word meaning one who lives alone? Not only had Merton chosen the monastic life, in his later years he requested complete solitude. He became a hermit. The man was protesting too much. He didn't want us to know how good it was, going all the way. He was guilty.

I knew I had one thing in common with Merton. We wrote books, we worked alone. In his "Author's Note" to *Seeds of Contemplation,* he had written, in the first sentence, no less: "This is the kind of book that writes itself almost automatically in a monastery." It was easy to crack the code; I knew why he had been seduced.

As we rolled through the gates of Mepkin Abbey, it was clear that I had not convinced Leonard Cunningham that I wasn't a prospect. He said, "In this place, a writer can cut his own course."

When you pass through you lose the familiar: the rural quiet you encounter at Mepkin Abbey is a thingish presence, the texture of all that can be experienced. You are disturbed by an infringing strangeness but you like it. You feel a hounding pressure which does not respect your peripheries—your famous need for strict autonomy. But you do not mind being dominated, robbed, or even, should it come to that, obliterated.

To pass through the gates is to move into "another intensity," a spreading flatland park of live oaks that dips suddenly into the waters of the Cooper, which run beside it for about three miles: brown and broad; imperceptible in its flow and impenetrable at its surface; a river reflecting light with a glare of such subtle sleight of hand that if you stand at the river's edge and a largemouth bass jumps close to you (this happened), before your eyes, all you will know is the huge dark sound of its belly-thunking reentry, and the deep rippling circles, traces of a thing which in southern lakes and rivers surpasses its defining form and becomes a tall tale. You miss the vision but have the experience.

But Mepkin Abbey is not a story about the flickering Big One that gets away. The story is true, but the point of Mepkin Abbey is that there is no story adequate to what occurred during those three days in late April of 1991. Mepkin Abbey welcomes no storyteller; it will not yield to sly narrative method, or maybe any other kind of method. At Mepkin Abbey, nothing happens.

We passed through—in early evening the gates would be closed and bolted—and pulled up to the guest dormitory: maximum accommodation, four retreatants. There were four of us, but I never saw anyone else enter or leave the premises. I heard muffled alarm clocks at 3:00 A.M., that's all. Leonard Cunningham showed me to the door and then that ebullient spirit of the highway said good-bye, turned and left, disappeared. I felt, at the time, that he left me too abruptly, even though I knew, at the time, that he hadn't.

I walked into an impression of strong alignments, an interior offering the pleasures appropriate to the perfect line and perfect angle. Structure and stillness. Is plane geometry an erotics for the ascetically inclined? Furniture embodying the idea of unobtrusiveness. In this place it would be difficult to recall decorative clutter. A simple crucifix over the bed. A room designed against distraction, for the better concentration on essential things. A meditator's base. I was in my room; the panic at the gas station was someone else's memory.

Two texts, placed on the small table, await me. Messages. A Bible, which I thumb but do not read, and a sheet of paper listing the undeviating schedule of the liturgical day, the ritual shaping of time toward the elegance of a Euclidean form, the sanctification of everyday life. At Mepkin Abbey they work against the trivial eventfulness of time, there being only one event, but the liturgy is not performed by angels. My primary intuition at Mepkin Abbey is of contemplation and its loss, and the work to recover, which is prayer. Prayer, says Merton, is the desire to pray.

If Merton is right, I have been praying for a long time. If what he says is true about writing contemplative books in a monastery, he knows exactly what sort of prospect he can seduce. Bad enough he has to write the phrase "writes itself"—I imagine myself a medium of the God of Writing who never revises. Cruelly, Merton finds it necessary to double my imagined pleasure. He has to say "almost automatically." I know how the qualifying "almost" plays into his hands. I know what he's implying: he's letting me think that I will be spared some self, granted an observation post, indulged sufficient self-consciousness to be the happy registrar of my happy experience at the happy scene of writing. I will not be required to surrender totally. Is this Merton's coded message? That the self can be preserved in a monastery? Will I be able, there, to stand on the border of self and no self? Is Mepkin Abbey the place, and is my room the room in which perfection finds "access to the page"? And I would survive to tell all and write prefaces to the world in which I, too, would say, "This is the kind of book that writes itself almost automatically in a monastery."

From my room at Mepkin Abbey I walk to the Cooper twice daily, once in late morning at eleven, and once in late afternoon at four, undeviatingly: my little addition to the liturgical life. So that I can loiter in the small and unpretentious graveyard where lie Henry R. and Clare Boothe Luce, and several of their relatives.

The quiet of Mepkin Abbey is at least partially a gift of the secular life that Henry R. Luce drove to economic perfection in his labors as publishing magnate. He was a major force in the Republican Party, she a major American convert to Catholicism who, in 1949, gave some 3,500 acres of their low country estate and antebellum rice plantation to those dedicated to creating a counterculture—a Trappist monastery being the only place in the world, said Merton on the day he died, in 1968, where communism works.

The tombstones have an unobstructed view down the slope to the river. Off to one side there is a black wrought-iron bench, which eased my low back pain, and which I would pull in front of the Luces, so that, my back to them, I could enjoy an unobstructed view of the river.

Once I saw a small heron stalk the edges of a backset. Another time a car moved slowly down the winding gravel road that passes about thirty yards off and dead-ends in a cul-de-sac. The car turned through the cul-de-sac and went back. Disappointed visitors to the Abbey, who came and left without leaving the car. Never saw me. Good they didn't leave the car. Women are welcome here. To make their retreats in a Trappist monastery. They have a special husband-and-wife cottage. Are they assuming abstention? The rhythm method? Are men now making retreats at convents? Across the river, about halfway, a powerful outboard, not that loud, dragging a water-skier, gone in five seconds. Luce should have bought the river.

I'm giving the impression that these little distractions preoccupied me. Mostly I sat there pleased with myself that I didn't care if I couldn't pray, or read the Bible, or have a serious memory, or a serious anything. That heron stalking the edge of the backset, walking away from me, head cocked, death eye staring fatally down into the shallows, I saw him several times. That was good. I was just loafing, I was "inviting my soul."

Boredom must be a familiar and welcome enemy at Mepkin Abbey, God's sly gift, the severe and necessary test of craft. Monasteries are places dedicated to banishing the distractions that keep us from facing up to what we are revealed to be in the times of our boredom. In the condition of true boredom, we have nothing left but ourselves. In the condition of true boredom, we are permitted perfect focus on the sound of our inner voice, in single-toned monologue, repeating itself. We become an emptiness no presence can fill. The monks face up to it; they have the craft; they have a 1,500-year tradition of discipline on their side. At Mepkin Abbey, I know nothing.

Leonard Cunningham told me they have 40,000 chickens, for the eggs. On my second morning, when I wasn't happily registering anything, when I felt private and autonomous, the chicken houses of Mepkin Abbey rescued me from the boredom which I could not distinguish from myself. Retreatants must not, however, wander over alone. The monks have put up a sign on the road to the farm saying so. Go ye to the church on your own, but go ye not to the farm. Expensive and dangerous machines; assembly lines; men at work whose distraction might be costly, and not just financially.

The monks who work the egg farm make real what the Luces made possible, Mepkin Abbey's exile society. The chicken houses sustain the community's spare material needs and its counterculture of monasticism. If the chicken houses should fail, these men go back to the parishes, to be who they are not. I needed a guide to the chicken houses and Father Aelred, the cantor—educated at the University of Virginia, a cherub out of the Italian Renaissance, far younger than me— agreed to take me over. A man I could imagine confessing to, and, a day later, in a sense, I did.

Bless me, Father, for I have sinned. O my God, I am heartily sorry for having offended Thee, and I detest all my sins. The pains of Hell. When I was less than a teenager, confession was coming out of church on a late Saturday afternoon having made a perfect Act of Contrition and having done my penance without a grudge and knowing with complete joy that should I be struck and killed by an automobile before I reached home I would go directly to Heaven, because God would find my soul beautiful. Now, at fifty, I think confession is telling who you are to someone who will not judge you a failure because you fail. To confess, to periodically relinquish privacy, to renounce solitude as an end in itself. It seemed a rehearsal for friendship; a discipline for community.

On the way to the chicken houses I asked Father Aelred to tell me what the Sacrament of Reconciliation was. I had seen the phrase in a brochure for retreatants given to me by Mike Baxter. If you wish to see a priest about a spiritual problem. If you wish to take the Sacrament of Reconciliation. "You knew it as confession," he said; he didn't add, "and that tells me how long you've been away." I said nothing. Reconciliation is not my problem; I've never been separated. I needed to confess. Not the sins, the sins are banal. The telling itself, last rites of absolution performed by and for the terminally hidden. "The terminally hidden": Truth or narcissism? Truth as narcissism? Those Brando movies of the fifties, which I took in in the fifties, exacting their price, now in my fifties? I am reluctant to confess, and a writer I admire tells me why. The confession may well be a plagiarism, marked by obvious suppressions.

Reading is the masturbation of my middle years. "My middle years" is a phrase of infinite hope. I read too much. Bless me, Father, for I have sinned.

The shocking thing about the chicken houses of Mepkin Abbey is that they are an extension of the aesthetic of Mepkin

Abbey. The monks can cause plane geometry to prevail even in a chicken house. It is a miracle of some magnitude that a place that has a natural right to violent stench has only a barely intolerable one. The chicken houses are actually clean.

Father Aelred was giving me the news about the chicken houses and the news was exceptionally good. The Mepkin Abbey egg is famous in South Carolina. The military bases demand it. The chickens are maximally productive; the chickens of Mepkin Abbey are happy. The egg farm will not fail because the farmers of Mepkin Abbey practice their art cunningly. Father Aelred is too modest to say that it doesn't hurt the business that the people know who cultivate those eggs. The romantic aura is intense; the people are swept away.

With the exception of the abbot, the cantor, the guest-master, and the very old, all the monks work the farm, but no more than a morning stint, four hours. Those with special skills in gardening, carpentry, automobile mechanics, and other arts pull less than a full shift. The afternoons are free for the pursuit of what monks pursue. Henry Luce would have been proud of this smashing venture in capital. Someone Luce abhorred said that in an economically just world we would work in the mornings and be free to pursue what we would pursue in the afternoons. Merton is right again, but there is one thing I will not do: I will not read his autobiography.

The schedule for retreatants says, *Rise 3:00 A.M.,* but I set my alarm for two-forty-five. Punctuality is my one undisputed virtue. The church is a five-minute walk. Time to shower and shave, but I take no chances. Cold water and toothpaste provide the required shock. I dress and walk fast and get there at three o'clock, twenty minutes before the praying of the first canonical hour. Two or three monks are already there.

The church is a long and narrow rectangle: at the far end the altar, at the other, the entrance, where, split by an aisle, there is a row of chairs for retreatants and day visitors. In front of this row a pew where a few monks sit, the ancient and the infirm. The choiring monks occupy the special pews facing each other on each of the long sides, about halfway between the entrance and the altar. Two pews on each side, each broken its entire length by small partitions that mark off individual spaces.

I sit invariably on the left side. I should chant and sing with the left side only, but it takes me a day to learn this. For the first day I chant and sing with both sides. The ancient and bent monks sitting near me are charitable; they find the places in the texts for me; they do not tell me to sing only with the left side. I must amuse them. Another enthusiastic retreatant. Tries to get here before us, chants all the time. Father Aelred sits alone, between the halves of the choir, in front of the retreatants, back to me, guitar in hand, poised, waiting for the knock that will announce *Vigils, 3:20.* It comes and he intones the first phrase in his warm and liquid tenor.

Vigils. We have come to the Lord's house; we are a gathering, keeping the watch with our nocturnal devotions while the world sleeps. We are diminished images of the angels, who need no sleep. We wait and watch for the light of the world.

I chant and sing with the monks, working hard to stay with the meaning of the texts, but the message is no match for the music. I lose the meaning so much the better to assume the music, the vocal timbres and ranges, which now, free of signification, enjoy an unimpeded path to me, their dominion.

4:00: Vigils end, Mass. I take the eucharist, actual bread, wine red and robust, burning its way down. I like the burning. Body and blood. I am not unreconciled, but I am unconfessed. Mortal sin. Why are adults standing in a circle? I am part of the circle, thinking about the circle. I will do it again, body and blood, next day, and a few hours before I must leave I will request to see Father Aelred, in guilt, who says, "Sometimes you have to work outside the system. You know the meaning later. It depends on what you do from here." I take him literally. "From here": Mepkin Abbey as the matrix of my future action, a burden I do not wish to contemplate.

4:45. Mass ends, lights are extinguished, and in the full dark, in the night's advancing chill, we begin the twenty-five-minute thanksgiving meditation. I am not ungrateful but I do not give thanks. I have no meditative subject, I attempt no directed thought, but the pictures come nevertheless, across an abyss, unsummoned but not unwelcome, of wife, children, parents, and friends. The unavoidables. I see them all as snapshots of fresh-faced classmates in a high school yearbook who do not deserve their fate. Their distance from me in this darkness is absolute but not terrifying. I think that they have escaped. I do not want to say that they have escaped from me. I try to gather these pictures to myself, these breathless faces, but they stay outside, like the dead.

5:20. The period of meditation is over, and we head directly to the dining hall where breakfast, like all meals at Mepkin Abbey, is taken in silence. Like dinner, which follows midday prayer at twelve-fifteen, breakfast is contiguous with a period of concentration and worship in church. We are not in church but I cannot tell the difference in mood or intention. Eating together—the monks and retreatants are separated by a folding partition, except for dinner, when I can eat and watch the monks at the same time—this, too, is liturgical. I'm hungry; I take communion again, this time without a twinge of guilt. Why do we require dinner conversation? In this silence, the surfaces of things give sufficient pleasure.

The partition is folded back and a six-foot lean man walks in wearing an apron and carrying a platter of scrambled eggs. Because at breakfast and supper I cannot enter the monks' dining hall to serve myself, he is here to serve me. He introduces himself in a voice just above a whisper as Brother Christian. He says something witty that I can't remember. I learn later that he was the abbot before the present abbot. The one before him, the first abbot of Mepkin Abbey, sits near me in church and finds my place in the texts. Another servant.

Brother Christian has the body of a miler. He used to be a canon lawyer. His wit doesn't subtract from his dour aspect, and I believe the man cannot lose an argument. He looks at my empty plate, points to his platter, and asks if I'd like "another shot." At my last vespers he will pass me a folded-up article from the *National Review* highly critical of my profession. I like his phrase "another shot" applied to scrambled eggs. I think he likes it too.

In my room I set my alarm for six-thirty. It is still dark.

In the church, at *7:00,* we celebrate *Lauds*: morning song, praise for the rising sun.

Mepkin Abbey wishes to confer upon me freedom to give everything to concentration, in a monastic time zone dedicated to intention pursued without impediment, to the eye fixed unwaveringly on the object. My failures during the praying of the liturgical hours are therefore obvious and easy to recall. My patience and my charity, unlike my punctuality, are not among my undisputed virtues, and they are pressed quickly to their limits: by the visiting soprano who, consistently, holds on to the last note of the last phrase, into the silence, a cloying sweetness of tone, just hanging there; by the possible novice, there to look and be looked over, a bass with a tin ear, who stands next to me for a day and assaults my pitch at every service. I imagine the two of us monks, assigned places in the choir next to one another, till death do us part. Water torture, a musical death sentence, and I know that I could not do it. To request a change of station would hurt him; I must request transfer to another abbey, Gethsemani. (I meet with our abbot, Father Francis. He tells me that my request for transfer requires a special dispensation from Rome. My case is doubtful, he says. I ask, respectfully, But why? In the kindest possible manner, Father Francis tells me that my case is trivial, that he will not put it forward.) And I am hurtled into boredom by readings from the Bible not done with keen attention to the aesthetic values of rhythm and sound. Unless they come across as beautiful performances of great writing, poetry, not conversation, I cannot, and do not, listen. Sensuous beauty is the first temptation, which I never refuse.

Thoughts of failure, the hubris of solitude, managed at a safe distance, in the reflective space of composition. At *Vespers* and *Compline,* the day's closing canonical hours, where the contemplation of the day should take place, and the sins of the word, deed, and the heart need to be reviewed, I do not contemplate and I do not review. "For the examination of past actions is a great help against falling into similar faults again." I must heed Scripture, but I do not heed Scripture: "Do not let the sun go down on your anger and give no opportunity to the devil. . . . Let all bitterness and wrath and anger be put away from you, with all malice, and be kind to one another, tenderhearted, forgiving one another, as God in Christ forgave you, for we are members of one another."

Vespers, evensong, *6:00* P.M.; *Compline,* complete, the last of the canonical hours, *7:35* P.M. I let the sun go down without self-examination; I do not ask forgiveness; I cannot feel myself a member. My kindness and tenderheartedness are without object, unless, perhaps, I am the object. Unless, perhaps, I forgive myself. The light falls and we must pray for protection against the night, but I do not pray for protection against the night because I do not feel the lurking threat. Compline is my treasured hour. The light falls and I feel whole. Let what will come, come. Compline, complete.

8:00 P.M. *Retire.*

Waiting for my flight back, I sit in a nearly deserted boarding area, thinking about reentry, thinking about taking

Mepkin Abbey back with me. I worry that Mepkin Abbey will break apart in the earth's atmosphere, burn up, become nothing. And then things go back to normal. Then I'm home.

Five months later, I run across this passage in Merton: "When a man enters a monastery he has to stand before the community, and formally respond to a ritual question: *Quid petis?* 'What do you ask?' His answer is not that he seeks a happy life, or escape from anxiety, or freedom from sin, or moral perfection, or the summit of contemplation. The answer is that he seeks *mercy*." I try to, but cannot imagine what the secular world would have to become for that ritual to obtain, for it to be one of ours.

2

We look for the resurrection of the dead, and the life of the world to come. —NICENE CREED

    Three weeks after my return from Mepkin Abbey I'm again on the way to the airport when my concentration gets diverted and something happens, but I'm of course prepared, which is the point of preparation pursued assiduously (I do not say fanatically), until it becomes a discipline of the unconscious, the true bulwark against disaster. Preparation like breathing: only death can part me from the practice.

    It's American on the way out, USAir on the way back, but I get it turned around. I don't make this kind of mistake. This is the kind of mistake that others make, especially those close to me. After a brief but terrible panic, during which my identity is sucked out, and I leave on the USAir ticket counter the sunglasses I wear 300 to 325 days per year, I catch the shuttle at Raleigh-Durham International and arrive, slightly triumphant, and slightly happy, at the proper terminal, sixty-two minutes before departure. Later, with my two pieces of luggage nicely stowed in the overhead compartment, and no one else's touching mine for the moment (things, we are warned, have a tendency to shift during flight), we push back from the gate, three minutes ahead of schedule.

There is nothing I can do about the tendencies behind the closed door of the overhead compartment. I get to airports one hour and thirty minutes in advance, this is what I can do, this is how I prepare.

Kennedy, first time, and I anticipate something glowing and dashing, a handsome airport, like the man it is named for. I walk, instead, through cramped spaces, dingy and vaguely dirty buildings built with relentless ignorance of all ideas of style, and a siege of bodies, many in urgent need of sunbathing. It isn't necessary for airports to look like this. Kennedy's ugliness (it pains me to have to phrase it that way) invades me, makes me fear my home is a mirage, and that when I return I will have to build everything over again, stone by stone, without help, in a strange land, not like an immigrant but like an exile.

Kennedy (that's better), the Aer Lingus terminal. Two Irish literary critics from University College, Dublin, men of seductive charm, will later claim, when I ask, that Aer Lingus means Air Line, and not, as I had hoped, Air Tongue. The midnight hours over the North Atlantic were in fact sexually uneventful, so I chalk up a point in their favor. Shortly after the captain turns off the FASTEN SEAT BELT sign in our 747, I flag down one of the sixteen female flight attendants and ask her the meaning of Aer Lingus. I ask her because I know she's been asked this question numerous times by inquisitive tourists, because I assume that those who train flight attendants for Aer Lingus anticipate that their charges will be so quizzed, and therefore prepare them with the correct answer. She replies quickly: "Fleet of Fish." I'm partially accepting because I know about lingcod, but suspect, immediately, that she must be partially wrong, because I'm convinced that *a-e-r* must be Irish for *a-i-r*. I resist concluding, however, that Aer Lingus means "Fleet of Air Fish," although I like the idea. Yet under no circumstances can I accept its plausibility. State institutions do not favor visionary phrasing, not even in the land of Yeats, Joyce, and Beckett, and Air Lingus is the airline of Ireland.

Of course, on the basis of such reasoning I mustn't accept "Air Line," either. The Irish authorities may have read early Yeats, but I do not suspect them of postmodernist wit. Since returning to the United States, I've learned that something called a lingthorn swims the seas, another point in favor of the female flight attendant.

Aer Lingus: lingus, linguistics, lingcod, lingthorn, linguine, and, yes, cunnilingus. The expert smiles a little when I ask, weeks later, if, in this instance, there is an etymological bridge between Irish and Latin. What about the Indo-European matrix, I say? Concerned for my embarrassment, the expert deftly alters the direction of our conversation.

Language, tongue, the study of tongues, tongue fish, little tongues of pasta, thorn tongues (pricklike), tongue of love, tongue in the air. What about the Indo-European matrix?

With the exception of "lingthorn," which I freely acknowledge I didn't know about until I returned, everything else plays through my mind on the flight out. A 747—to this point I'm a jumbo jet virgin—is so big I feel only an agreeable sensation of floating in the thing whose name I may not understand. Playing with the possibilities of "lingus" yields agreeable sensation—I do not speak hyperbolically, I mean erotic lift—a floating at another level, inside the floating thing, my body inside my mind, lithesome comrade of my speculations.

When I return from Ireland I decide that the Irish literary critics of seductive charm were either wrong or that they were playing with me. Which, I can't determine. They studied Irish all those years in school and didn't learn *lingus,* or were putting me on, deadpan. I'll never know, because I'll never ask. I'll never ask because I don't wish to know.

When I return I learn that *lingus* is the noun form of an Irish verb meaning to skip, to dart, to go away. I learn that there is a lingbird. (I like to imagine its moves.) I read that *ling* is the name of a fish (this I knew) three to four feet long (this I didn't know) swimming the seas of Northern Europe, definitely around Ireland (this also I didn't know). I'm beginning to think that the female flight attendant was close to the truth. I learn that in English "ling" is archaic for the act of putting out one's tongue. The *Oxford English Dictionary* gives an illustration that I like: "Her tongue would ling out from her mouth." A tongue in the air, darting. "Ling out" is spectacular. I'm beginning to think that I'm close to the truth, too, and that the truth is a little bawdy, as it should be.

The hidden connections among things. They don't necessarily constitute a conspiracy of malignant intent. They may present an opportunity for an imagination not necessarily sick. I practice interpretation on the principle of suspicion, not because I am necessarily paranoid, but because I am a reader and lead a textual life, because I swim in textual seas of written tongue.

This trip isn't my idea; this trip is her idea. Circumstances make it impossible for us to take our first European vacation, or any vacation, together. I tell her I have to have one, bad. She says, Why not go alone? I reply, What a shocking idea! She says, That's why you should do it. I'm acting a little, trying out a line a little. I like to act. As I say, What a shocking idea!, as I begin to propel the words from my mouth, as they start to skip off my tongue, I'm sincere, completely so, but as the sentence forms, when it's finished, I'm no longer sincere. I'm delivering a line, behind which I hide, thrilled by what I know I am going to do, though I don't tell her my secret until the next day.

Things are being arranged. The next day—I haven't told her yet—she claims to have been in the vicinity of our travel agency, so she gets me an itinerary for what she believes are likely dates, in May, which turn out, naturally, to be right.

The ticket is in the computer. All I need do is call and accept. Or not. As I wish.

I used to travel too much, almost always in connection with lecturing. Then I stopped. Now I'm traveling again, in connection with I don't know what. I think I linged out to Ireland.

She is asked, by a mutual friend, Who does Frank know in Ireland? She replies, correctly, Yeats.

Long after she has heard me on *lingus,* she (who writes fiction) tells me the story of the Celtic creation myth. She claims she heard it from a woman, an obscure poet. The sea god Lir (so it goes) needed help from those he had created, in order to finish the job. Because he had only half a tongue. The experts cannot verify my wife's tale.

When I return I consult a dictionary of Indo-European roots. I find *ling* and its cognates in Old High German, Old English, West Germanic, Dutch, Middle English, Low German, Greek, and, yes, Latin: long, elongate, lunge, prolong; to grow longer, to yearn for. The Latin cognate, they say, is *longus.* They don't mention the obvious: *lingus* or *lingua.* Whether this is the result of ignorance or shyness, I do not know. They miss altogether the Celtic and Gaelic forms, and, knowing that women have tongues, too, refuse to mention that *ling* is Sanskrit for penis. Nevertheless, the deep structural coherence of the Celtic, Germanic, Italic, and Greek branches of Proto-Indo-European is apparent to me. The resemblances cannot be accidental, though the experts will claim otherwise. Thus:

long
darting
fish
tongue
language

A fishing tongue, slender, three to four feet long, imagine it, darting, performing words of love. The Indo-European mother. What carried me to Ireland, yearning?

These are the pages I prefer not to write. I could have given a hint a few pages back, deferred it, hinted again, deferred again. Then given it all, wide open. Narrative technique as cocktease. But I didn't because I have no control over the material. I desire to sink it into a darkness so deep that I could never drag it to light, forget so perfectly that the work of forgetting will leave no scar, but I cannot do it. By narrative rights this part should have come earlier. If I wait any longer, it can't come out at all in this meditation, and yet I will not have forgotten. I will have failed twice, once as a writer, once as a represser.

Something else happens, but this time I cannot be prepared because I'm ignorant of the interiors of 747s. I arrive at the Aer Lingus terminal, 4:50 P.M. Stand at the end of an immense line, clogged with luggage. No problem, two hours and ten minutes to departure. The problem awaits me at the

other end, at the counter, where the Aer Lingus clerk an-
nounces, tactlessly, that I must check both bags. I'm hit by a
panic worse than the first, accompanied by an impulse to do
violence, not necessarily to the Aer Lingus clerk, though she's
an inviting target. The choice is to go forward, on her terms,
or to say fuck Ireland and go back to North Carolina. I don't
give a shit anymore. The ticket, $788, is nonrefundable, but I
don't give a shit anymore.

I relax. I'm going back. I say to the clerk, in the natural
voice of a corpse, that my travel agent assured me I was allowed two carry-ons. I don't remind her of what might happen if I check my bags. I'm hoping that she thinks she's
looking at a maniac. She replies in an automatic voice, nicely
covering her fear, that the big one will not fit in the overhead
compartment. She knows this. The smaller one, maybe, I
could take a chance. They'll have to check it for me if it
doesn't fit, at the gate, the last minute, it might not get on, she
guarantees nothing. Her response enrages me. I detect an in-
finitesimal smirk. She's not afraid. I will need to take this
scene to another level. A 747, she is saying in so many words,
has an overhead compartment smaller than those on planes in
the low 700s, one of which I flew into Kennedy and which
accommodated my luggage so graciously in its overhead
compartment.

The big one contains my clothes. Fuck my clothes. The
smaller one contains my hefty leather jacket, a sweater, my
toiletries, the complete poems of Yeats, a selected but very
full edition of Wallace Stevens, Eliot's *Four Quartets,* Thomas
Merton's *The Sign of Jonas,* a massive history of Ireland, hardcover, which outweighs easily all the other books put to-

gether, three pens, three pencils, two writing tablets (legal size), my passport, a pair of shoes, a small umbrella, and the growing manuscript of a personal meditation prompted by my visit to America's most obscure Trappist monastery, Mepkin Abbey—a new departure for me in writing, an obsession with Catholic solitude that I could not leave home. The momentum was good, it was going to happen, I was going to like it. I could not let them get their hands on this bag. This I could not permit. Did not the scribe-monks who labored in the scriptoria of the monasteries and monastic schools devote perfection of care to the manuscripts they were entrusted to reproduce? I was exhibiting monastic, not paranoid, behavior.

I decide to take a chance. I cannot explain why. First they weigh the big bag and then they check the big bag. Who cares. I feel myself leave the edge. I cannot explain why. For some reason I don't remember that I'd made a photocopy of the manuscript before I left and had put it in a fireproof box, a filing cabinet. Years ago, when I had frightening problems, I used to use the refrigerator. I remember the photocopy as I walk forever to the boarding area. I'm elated by the recollection. I don't glow with embarrassment because nobody knows me here. Am I a maniac? Do I look like a maniac?

In the boarding area I scope out the carry-on luggage of those near me, hoping for pieces bigger than mine, carried by Irish nationals who ought to know better. I see a guy with four carry-ons, none of them that big, but four is arrogant. I can tell by his shirt and hat that he's Irish. I sit across from two young women. Brogues. I ask them out of the blue if they were given trouble about their carry-ons, which they most definitely should have been. They say no and look at me. I decide not to ask them if I can measure my luggage against theirs, put it right alongside. They would think me a pervert, they would have me arrested, the police would not let me bring my bag into my cell. I imagine asking, Just the manuscript? They say, No. I say, Why not? They say, For the same reason we won't let you have your belt. In my fantasy I forget, again, about the photocopy.

Time to board. A joke. They don't care what we bring on. They don't hassle the Irish guy, they don't look at my bag, they barely look at me: my ticket hand, the ticket, the boarding pass, that's it. The overhead compartment is shockingly small, but I get it in without too much forcing. I sit in my aisle seat, happy. I get up, open the compartment door, and without bringing the bag down, pull out a tablet and a pen. I intend to work on the monastery piece once we take off. I'm at the point where I pass through the gates of Mepkin Abbey. I feel the manuscript in there, though I can't quite see it. I close the door. I feel a little crazy, but I'm pretty happy. The takeoff is like nothing. I think about *aer lingus* and write sentences about Mepkin Abbey. I write one about Merton that makes me smile amidst strangers.

Halfway there I have to take a leak. It comes to me that I won't be able to watch my overhead compartment from the restroom, but I can't hold it for another three hours and twenty-eight minutes. I consider leaving the restroom door open and leaning way back while I take a leak. This is an idea that could get me arrested. I have written two new pages on this flight, unphotocopied. Do 747s have fax machines? Dick in hand, I worry about my writing. When I get back to my seat I go straight for the bag. Put it across the seat with great awkwardness. Take the manuscript out, look at it, flip through the pages, making sure they're all there.

When the Aer Lingus 747 pushed back from the gate at Kennedy at 7:00 P.M., I set my watch the appropriate five hours in advance. One hour and thirty minutes later they dim the lights and show a movie. I was exhausted but couldn't sleep, and stared at the screen stupidly and unwaveringly, for some reason not plugging in my earphones. I was taking in a movie I knew nothing about, not having read the reviews, with the great French actor Gérard Départment, and the erratic, the critically abused Andie MacDowell, who has recently surprised her severest reviewers, and therefore has become an item of interest, something of a small mystery, this ex-model.

In frequent and often pointless close-ups of the American actress (planned for beauty and no other reason), something breaks through my torpor which isn't rooted in her beauty. Through the arresting flesh I see the skeletal structure of her face. I must be watching some other movie.

The great French actor is subtle, and without sound the great French actor is of no interest. She makes him disappear. The meticulous realist sets dissolve in her presence. There is only Andie MacDowell but there is no Andie MacDowell. She is a series of rapidly changing and shocking masks, an actress in a nonnaturalist theater, set in a 747, at 37,000 feet, with an audience of one. I think Andie is inhabited. The names I attach to what crosses through her and into me are trivial. The names are nothing. In the grip of such theater I become diffident to the fate of manuscripts.

When I return to the United States, I read an essay by Yeats on Noh theater containing this sentence: "It is even possible that being is only possessed completely by the dead."

The Gresham Hotel, Dublin. As I register, the son of a bitch of a bellhop tries to pick up my bags. I bark. He puts them down quickly but gently. I'm twice his size.

My room, midmorning, no sleep all night and I drop off, dead, then suddenly alive in the sound of a key, a turning door knob, someone trying to get in, getting in. I let something out with operatic force. For two days I have a raw throat. Son of a bitch of a housekeeper. Claims she made a mistake.

The central streets of Dublin, a kind of hallucination: the Municipal Gallery (or is it Yeats's mournful "The Municipal Gallery Revisited," which?), the Liffey (Joyce's river), Trinity College, Grafton Street, St. Stephen's Green (and the other Stephen), again Grafton Street (Bloom is here), St. Patrick's (Swift is the dean), the General Post Office, headquarters of the Irish Nationalists during the Easter Rising of 1916, property of Patrick Pearse and the other rebel leaders, and Yeats:

> *When Pearse summoned Cuchulain to his side,*
> *What stalked through the Post Office?*

I walk these streets of Dublin, through Irish texts, happy in my self-consciousness. In the lift and swirl of sensation, stillness at the center: I am buoyed, buoyed up (by whom or what?), a body like an engine so efficient that with minimal expression of energy it does all the work it's called upon to do, powering me effortlessly through streets and dense crowds, slicing through, sailing in a brisk and steady wind. Doing this is a pleasure, knowing this pleasure is a greater pleasure. This is easy, this I could do forever, "in and out of the game." It's even possible that being is only possessed by dead writers. When I summon Yeats to my side, what stalks through the central streets of Dublin? When I give dead writers the gift of continuing life, do they give me the greater gift of some other kind of existence, which must not be called life?

In the evenings, very late, I return to the Gresham to work on the monastery manuscript, the loving memory of my solitude. Before I turn out the lights, I place it in its proper place, in the small bag. In the mornings, when I leave for the day, I arrange the straps on the small bag in a precise and odd pattern, so that when I return that evening, late, to work again on the manuscript, I will know instantly if someone has tampered with my small bag, at my haunted Gresham, with Joyce's Gabriel just down the hall, his lust rebuffed, his wife yielding to the memory of a dead man, and Gabriel and me taking it all in.

Dublin, the Abbey Theatre.
In the lobby, in the halls, in the stairwells, in the bar:

paintings of the founders and the benefactors, the playwrights and the actors of early Abbey history. "Around me the images . . . An ambush."

In honor of the seventy-fifth anniversary of the Easter rebellion, on the main stage, Sean O'Casey's *The Plough and the Stars,* which I cannot absorb. In the laboratory theater, daring, Thomas Murphy's *The Patriot Game,* which invades me.

The two Irish literary critics, men of seductive charm, one the son of a former amateur heavyweight boxing champion of Northern Ireland, grief-struck and funny (this is Seamus Deane); the other, urbane and amused (this is Kevin Barry, rebel namesake, ghost-bearer). We talk at length, in technical detail, of boxers and of Thomas Murphy. When Murphy gets it going, they tell me, he's tough to beat. When I return to the United States, I ask several people of the theater what they think of Thomas Murphy. They haven't heard of him. He's been writing plays for thirty years. A friend, America's last Marxist, may be right: Ireland is a Third World country. He hasn't heard of Murphy either, and he's heard of everything.

The Patriot Game is set in the present. A group of young actors learns about the rebellion by improvising a play about it. They take the parts of the major figures. At first skeptical, then drawn, then gripped by the dead. No sets, no props, no music. It's like these people walked in off the street. This is happening, the dead are speaking.

I shall arrange a meeting of Andie MacDowell and Thomas Murphy. She will be his Maud Gonne, he her William Butler Yeats. She will be taken by him in all ways but one. She, the woman loved but not won. They shall be permitted a brief affair. She shall suffer it in stride, he with lifelong distraction. She shall marry some drunken lout—call him MacBride—who shall perform a political act none thought him capable of: "changed, changed utterly / A terrible beauty is born." Seamus Deane will write the poem. Kevin Barry will attempt to teach this poem. He begins by reading it to his class. He reads so well that there is nothing left to say.

I shall arrange a meeting of Andie MacDowell and Thomas Murphy, of Thomas Murphy and Maud Gonne, of Andie MacDowell and William Butler Yeats. And they shall contract terminal passion. And then the dead shall speak.

The Irish guy with the four carry-ons was friendly. We talked. He claimed he had a good time visiting his relatives in Spanish Harlem. Without transition he told me that I'd never need to worry about crime in Ireland. Except for one thing. Outside of Dublin, said this Dubliner, people steal things out of cars, they break in if they see anything worth taking. Don't leave anything in the car. I forget to ask him about the trunk. Do they speculate on trunks? Can they tell a rental car in a glance? Seeing nothing inside, break the window, open the door, rip out the backseat, smash through the partition, gain access to the trunk, hiding place of the big bag and the small bag? Wasn't the partition made of metal? It seemed like an awesome length to go to on speculation, but the poverty in the beautiful countryside is serious. Would they rifle through the two bags on the spot, get the good stuff, then leave? Or would they take the bags somewhere (this is what they would do), then take the good stuff, then throw the bags down some hole where they would never be found?

After four and a half days in Dublin I'm to pick up my compact rental car at the airport, for my sojourn to the west of Ireland, to see Yeats. On my second day in Dublin I decided to prepare. What, really, do they mean by a compact here? My two bags together will not take up that much space, but what if the trunk of a compact in Ireland is analogous to an overhead compartment on an Aer Lingus 747? I call the rental agency on my second day. I consider their answer to my question unclear. I invent a strategy: put the small bag in the trunk, the big bag on the backseat, do not lock the car. Suck them in. They will be too thrilled with an easy heist to go through the trouble of ripping out the backseat, smashing through the metal partition, stealing the small bag, which, of course, they would be speculating was in there. I like the strategy. I invent a brilliant refinement: even if the trunk can accommodate both bags, I shall place the big bag on the back-seat and "forget" to lock the car. Totally deceive the fuckers. Or should I leave both bags on the backseat, remove the man-uscript alone, place it in the trunk, with the car unlocked? This is the final refinement, and I have to say that I like it, very much. There is, of course, a bit of a risk involved, even in this scenario, and I begin to wonder if the rubber covering the floor of the trunk might be ever so subtly lifted, the man-uscript lovingly inserted, spread out with care, leaving no tell-tale signs of unevenness. Or should the manuscript simply be left on the front seat, utterly exposed, a thing too absurd to steal?

I pick up my car. A Ford Fiesta. New, spotless in and out, fire engine red, so much the better to be noticed. Both bags fit in the trunk, but this solves no problem of mine. I get in, back out of the parking space, and begin to roll slowly toward the exit. Approximately ten yards later, I stop, get out, walk to the back of the car, in order to check the trunk, in order to give it a violent upward jerk. It holds.

Sligo, the haunted territory of Yeats, four hours away.

I ease the pain by driving to Sligo without stopping, check into a clean and cozy bed-and-breakfast, lock the luggage in my room (but not before arranging the straps on my small bag in a precise and odd pattern), then head out for Lissadell House. The proprietor of the bed-and-breakfast, helpful and kindly and a little frightened (do I look like a maniac?), tells me that the public is not allowed into Lissadell on Sundays, the family's one day off. But I have no need to enter.

The drive to Lissadell House is about six miles, circuitous, on three little-used roads, the last rarely traveled. At the end, I drive through a small wood, into a clearing, a sudden expanse of lawn, and there it is: the house that inspired Yeats's bitter and moving late elegy, "In Memory of Eva Gore-Booth and Con Markiewicz." The Gore-Booths of Lissadell House, Eva and Constance, the sisters of Yeats's meditation on social change, "both / Beautiful, one a gazelle."

I had seen Con Markiewicz, the actress, only two nights before, in Dublin, at the Abbey, in *The Patriot Game,* the woman who had been jailed for her part in the Easter Rising, condemned to death, the sentence lifted. Con has changed. She is no longer beautiful. She is not now a gazelle, if ever she was. She's sturdily built, in her mid-twenties this time, a robust athlete who can take physical punishment, whatever the authorities would like to dish out. She gives no quarter, she is fierce and fanatical. In the play's closing seconds, fist raised in defiance, her thrilling full-throated outburst—Up the Republic!—shakes the roof and everyone in the house. I go shocked into the street, walk back to the Gresham, thinking, Write to Con, encourage her to take a warm drink of water, lemon juice, and honey before each performance. To protect the voice, because we need that voice.

I went to Lissadell House to see the poem, not the house:

> *The light of evening, Lissadell,*
> *Great windows open to the south, . . .*

There it is, 7,500 square feet, with ease. Great windows, more than four dozen, five feet wide by twelve feet high, with ease, two floors' worth, filmed over. The stone of Lissadell blackened with mildew: at the top, streaked with bird shit. The surviving Gore-Booths are barely hanging on. It would take a fortune to keep those windows as Yeats had seen them. Numerous fortunes to blast those stones clean.

The inside I didn't wish to see. I had seen and smelled enough of such interiors in the fiction of Faulkner. Interiors of the comatose. Windows opened no more, trapping the air of generations; the heavy draperies and furniture absorbing and preserving the odors of generations; decaying carpets; the stinking flesh of the old who have given up; motes of dust turning in the sunlight; deep layers of soot, thickened and hardened over the years into genuine soil, coating the top ledges of paintings too numerous to count; a motif of elegant filth, stench, rot. This I didn't want to see.

I go to Lissadell to see the poem. I do not want the house, but the house wants me. I want "the light of evening, Lissadell." I walk the grounds slowly. In the end, it's the poem, in a photo finish.

Driving back to Sligo from Lissadell House, close to town I see a sign for Drumcliff. Yeats is buried in the churchyard there:

> *Earth, receive an honored guest:*
> *William Yeats is laid to rest.*

"The words of a dead man," Auden had written in his elegy for Yeats, "Are modified in the guts of the living." He "became his admirers." Yeats as me. Who do I become? Is it necessary that I have an "I"?

Late at night, in Sligo, writing the monastery piece, I have friendly jousts with Thomas Merton. He tells me that Saint Anthony says that in perfect prayer the contemplative "no longer realizes that he is praying or indeed that he exists at all." I have been perhaps foolish to resist. In the condition

of perfect contemplation I shall have no manuscript to protect, because no self. No self, no need to prepare against disas-
ter. I shall have nothing, I shall be nothing. Preparation like
breathing: only death can part me from the practice. Or God,
or art. The extinguishment of all the conditions of selfhood.
Appetite, will, interest, gone. The mania of my paranoia,
gone. The blood relations, the friends, and the spouse, for
whom you can never prepare, and likely would not even if
you could—gone. To relinquish; to become a capacity for
reception, purely.

The architecture of Drumcliff is a rebuke to the world.
An eloquent severity of style, for the simplicity of God.

To stand before Drumcliff, to fix it with undeviating
gaze, and in rapt attention obliterate all distance, under a cold
gray sky in late autumn, in a gauntness of landscape, in a
steady harsh wind, becoming the object of my vision.

A day later, Galway.

I walk into Ireland's most noble bookstore, in order to
buy a play by Thomas Murphy called *The Gigli Concert,* and
there he is, in photographic transubstantiation, America's
monk of writing, Don DeLillo, eyes wide, obsessed, commanding; the gaze to the camera dead on—in the camera,
through the camera, out the other side—fixated on some object elsewhere at some other plane. The gaze that hails. I must
inform him:

**URGENT STOP NEED DRUMCLIFF VISION STOP
SEND THE GAZE STOP IMMEDIATELY**

If he sends The Gaze, in appreciation I shall arrange a meeting in New York of Don DeLillo and William Butler Yeats, in the Bronx, on Arthur Avenue, at Dominick's. DeLillo will order the linguine with clams and the arugula salad. Yeats, uncharacteristically unnerved, by the Bronx confused, does not order. DeLillo tells the waiter—an impatient Italian-American stud—that the gentleman would enjoy the same. Yeats relaxes, regains his patrician manner, and commences to speak with his usual, outrageous artificiality. "DeLillo," he says, "I have the highest regard for your black leather jacket and would be pleased to have one for myself, so that I, too—with impunity, sir—might walk the streets of your Bronx."

Murphy's play is about an unfulfilled self-made man who wants to sing like a great Italian tenor, like Beniamino Gigli.

From Galway I drove south to Yeats's tower, Thoor Ballylee, and then from there the few kilometers over to Coole Park. The day after I did that, I did it again, step for step.

Each morning of my sojourn in the west of Ireland it happens. In my bed-and-breakfast, arise, pack the few things I've removed from my luggage the night before, check the manuscript in the small bag: take it out, look at it, make sure all the pages are there, in order, put it back in, zip it up in its special side compartment. Go to the dining room, making sure to lock the door of my room. Try it after I lock it. Rattle it. Return, after breakfast, brush my teeth, put away the toiletries. I can't remember. Check the small bag. The manuscript. Ready. Go to the front desk with the big bag and the small bag. Put them down in front of me, between me and the front desk. Pick them up, return to the room, check to see if something was left behind. Return to the front desk with the big bag and the small bag. Put them down in front of me, between me and the front desk. Pay the bill. The car. Put the bags down in front of me, between me and the trunk. Open the trunk, put the bags in. I can't remember. Check the small bag. The manuscript. Close trunk, start car, shut off motor, go to trunk, I can't remember. The small bag, the manuscript. Shut trunk, try it, with a violent upward jerk, trying to remember. I think I remember. Start car and motor down highway. Pull over. The trunk, a violent upward jerk. Am I remembering? Start car, shut off motor. The trunk, I can't remember, the small bag, the manuscript, the pages, in order. Shut trunk start car I can't remember. Is it safe? Do it again, can't remember. Drive off in despair, not remembering.

The day before I left Dublin, to go to the west of Ireland, I visited the tower Joyce lived in for a few days as a young man, site of the first chapter of *Ulysses*. Now called the Joyce Tower, a little museum, full of the dead man's effects.

Sometimes called the Martello Tower, because designed by some Italian so named, and erected, in the days of the Napoleon scare, all over the coasts of Ireland. Perhaps forty feet high, the mountains rising behind, Dublin Bay all before it.

I went there with three students. Steve Newman, one of mine, from Duke, spending a semester at University College, Dublin: shy, vastly read, a poet, physique of a serious bodybuilder. Two graduate students from University College, Dublin: John Redmond, another namesake, quiet, stylishly dressed, who smiles a little when I tell him that I saw him and Con in *The Patriot Game* the night before; and Patrick O'Sullivan, from the countryside, who has by heart the best passages of the known and unknown poets in the English language. I don't mean one or two lines. I mean passages.

Before we go to the tower, we hike in the mountains for more than two hours, talking literature and words all the way, O'Sullivan leading the seminar, Redmond and Newman chipping in once in a while. O'Sullivan sees me make a note—I must have thought of something for the monastery piece—and he says, *"ciotóg."* Irish for a left-hander, he tells me. I ask him if the word has the usual connotations. Yes, he says. Off center. I tell him that in Italian the word for left hand is the word for sinister. *La mano sinistra.* Redmond appears to like that. Newman makes a note, then this shy fellow informs me that it's an excellent thing to do it in a jacuzzi. He tells me that I should try it, as if he knows that I haven't.

At the tower, the best place is the top, gun rest still there, long views, good air. The first page of *Ulysses.* Which one of us is Buck Mulligan? Which Stephen? Newman or Redmond could do Stephen, with ease. It's obvious that O'Sullivan is Mulligan. So who will I be? I want to be Bloom, but he doesn't appear on the first page.

I say to no one in particular that my father's father, Augusto Lentricchia, a poet and anarchist, who couldn't work in the Depression with six children to feed, used to subscribe to a radical newspaper called *Il Martello,* the hammer. Then I say that my mother's father, Tomaso Iacovella, politically conservative, who worked all the time, and told stories all the time—fables, he used to call them, satirical and bawdy—once taught me an Italian slang word for penis. Guess what it was? *Il martello!* Redmond actually laughs out loud. *Il martello,* I say again, and I try to say it the way Tomaso said it. I try to mime his tone, his look, what he did with his hands. I try to become my mother's father.

We didn't but we could have, we should have resurrected Molly Bloom herself, right there. We could have told her about *ciotóg* and the jacuzzi and Aer Lingus and *il martello.* Boys, she says. Yes, we say. Do what my cracked husband likes to do best, she says. What's that, Molly, we say. Kiss my ass, she says. At which point O'Sullivan pulls his most astounding feat of literary memory and says, That's not you, Molly. This is you: "any man thatd kiss a womans bottom . . . hed kiss anything unnatural where we havent 1 atom of any kind of expression in us all of us the same 2 lumps of lard before ever I do that to a man pfooh the dirty brutes the mere thought is enough." That's you, Molly, O'Sullivan says. "Kiss my ass," Molly, is not you.

Boys, she says.

yes we say yes we will Yes.

3

I seemed to be the same person, and I was the same person, I was still myself, I was more myself than I had ever been, and yet I was nothing. —THOMAS MERTON

I wish that I could say that it wrote itself, but New York wrote it. —CAPTION, *NEW YORKER* CARTOON

The day after I returned from Ireland I plunged back into the monastery writing, finishing it in a week. Two weeks later I was doing it again, this time it's the Irish trip, and the sentences come almost without trying. By mid-July I finish and here comes the anxiety for more, I was mainlining it, I had to have it, there wasn't any more, but I manage, just barely, to distract myself with preparations for an impending, extended, and much longed-for dislocation from home. But the preparations went too quickly and I couldn't pull myself apart from myself. My stash was gone.

Then, a week after moving to New York, where for the fall semester of '91 I'm to direct a Duke University program for seniors interested in literature and the other arts, a letter arrives from Mark Edmundson of the University of Virginia. He asks me if I'd like to write something for a volume that Viking will be publishing on the "current state of literary studies," a presentation of my side in response to numerous harsh attacks on the academy, where I reside in partial beatitude. No, I wouldn't. Then, page two, and a first-order temptation: Edmundson tells me that it would be desirable if I could write a "brief intellectual autobiography that would somewhere contain a statement of my present allegiances. The piece could be quite personal, a chance for some self-reflection." I can't resist, I say yes, not too eagerly, I hope. But I don't tell Edmundson that I don't, anymore, know what my allegiances in literary criticism are, or what my "position" is, as they say, or that I'll try self-reflection with the desire not to have a self to reflect upon. I don't tell him that I'd like to mix up the personal and the intellectual to the point where it would be impossible to separate them, not as an exercise in high-wire theory (this I know how to do), but as an act of homage to the real state of my affairs.

Some of my students are going to have trouble adjusting to New York. My wife, no question. But not me. People I've met from other parts of the country think I'm from the city itself. Queens, I was once told by a woman who grew up in Queens. The misidentification thrills me, and a couple of times I don't bother to correct the mistake. I think I learned to sound the way I sound because as a teenager in the 1950s I lived in *On the Waterfront*. I learned to sound the way a real man sounds, tough (I'm not, of course, referring to Italian-American manhood, another level altogether), but not tough you-know-where. The Brando character in *Waterfront* is a cliché I like to draw tightly around me.

I've been coming here regularly since the fifties for weekends; now I'm becoming a member of my heart's second home, the first one being Hillsborough, North Carolina, a village of 3,000. On my second day, I tell someone who thinks I'm making a radical change that it isn't so. Because, I say, Manhattan and Hillsborough are the same. I shall pay for saying this, pay double for writing it—two islands of tranquility necessary for writing, the former more peaceful even than the latter. Manhattan is where walking the streets I lose the "I" easily, in two seconds, and sentences and phrases come into me, shape themselves as forms of sensation, good stuff, keepers, like Wordsworth peripatetic, composed, in the Lake District composing, me on Seventh Avenue South, through the gates.

I'm not supposed to be doing this, I'm supposed to be writing the last chapter of my never-ending book on modernism, I'm supposed to be writing on T. S. Eliot. The day after I say yes to Mark Edmundson, I write in my little red notebook: "My Kinsman, T. S. Eliot." I wonder how I could explain that to my parents (answer: I'll never bring it up), who moved into my mother's father's house when I was in single digits, where we lived until I was twenty-one. Three generations of Italians in a two-family house on Mary Street. How would I explain that to my grandparents, all four of whom lived into my early thirties? Eliot, my kinsman, from St. Louis, a premier WASP who went to Harvard, then to England for good, where he took on a different sound, like a complete Englishman. Absurd.

I admit that I can see a fragile connection. We both wanted to sound like somebody else. But I never wanted to sound like Eliot. In my neighborhood? And we were both drawn to acting. Theater as the medium of our kinship. What did we sound like originally? Is that a relevant question? I don't want to get into it. Maybe the connection isn't so fragile. Maybe we'd prefer not to remember, because maybe we'd prefer not to know what we know.

My allegiance is not to a literary theory but to the sum total of my liberating literary experiences, and, I have told you, have I not, what I want liberating from. Most of these experiences are text-triggered, but not all. Most of the triggering texts are what a literary culture less guilty than ours used to call "great," "major," and "classic," but not all. I take my liberation where I find it. When I say "but not all" I give the impression that I like the performing and visual arts, which I do, but that's not what I was thinking about. I was thinking about experiences whose sources virtually none would call "art" or "aesthetic," which most would call "life." The art and life distinction, so venerable and so important, makes "life" harder for me. I can't exactly say to hell with the distinction because I half believe in it. The fun is all in disrespecting it by finding art in life, or, if you can't, by making it up in concert with the givens, the gifts, which need to have

their say—a desire we ought to respect. The ethics of interpretation: Be decent to your materials.

Is it becoming obvious to you that I'm a somewhat un-
easy Italian-American aesthete who finds Walter Pater, un-
official mentor of Oscar Wilde, almost sufficient? "Of this
wisdom, the poetic passion, the desire for beauty, the love of
art for art's sake has most; for art comes to you professing
frankly to give nothing but the highest quality to your moments as they pass, and simply for those moments' sake."
When I experience art, I feel good because I feel the specificity of the moment, the act, the image, the scene, but before
and after I don't feel too good, so I seek out more experiences
of art's particularity because art is the only place I know
where to find deliverance of the specific from the habits of
abstraction. Pater means "art" in the traditional sense, a good
enough sense. But if I limit myself to what he intends, I don't
feel good that often. That's why I look for the beautiful everywhere, why I coax and stroke it when I find it stirring in
front of me. And I do mean "in front of me," in a restaurant
in Little Italy, 146 Mulberry Street (honor to the site), at Angelo's (everything's in a name). Art as stubborn specificity, as
untheorizable peculiarity. Art for life's sake.

I had walked down to Angelo's from Bleecker and Carmine, where I attended *la messa Italiana* at Our Lady of Pompeii, sparsely populated by retired immigrants who take me
back to Utica's east side, the world of my grandparents, St.
Anthony's on St. Anthony Street, one of Utica's three Italian
churches. There it is: the same elaborate imitation Renaissance interior, with a ceiling after Michelangelo's Sistine
Chapel, the Italian women, old, in black, severely devoted,

the affectless manner of the priest droning formulas, and the same old me, disconnected, cold. I was looking for something good I thought I had met six months before, at Mepkin Abbey, then met again, four Sundays in a row, at Holy Family, a Catholic church in Hillsborough that looks as if it should have been a subject for a photograph by Walker Evans, like the one captioned "Wooden Church for Blacks, South Carolina, 1936." In Evans's photo: weather-beaten raw wood, dried to a crisp, flaking and warping under mean sunlight, a child's stick drawing of a house with a tiny bell tower perched on the peak above the front face, saying this is a church. Holy Family doesn't look like the church in the Evans photo but it has a tendency, and someday, when the funds fail completely, that's what it will look like, and then it will have fulfilled its architectural and religious promise. In its shocking plainness it will become essence of church, the aesthetic and spiritual negation of Our Lady of Pompeii and St. Anthony's. The American-Protestant half of my soul is getting the best of the Italian-Catholic half. (What is a church supposed to look like, anyway?) At Our Lady of Pompeii I am myself. I cannot give in and had no expectation that at Angelo's I'd meet again what I thought I had found at Mepkin Abbey.

What happens is a continual surrender of himself as he is at the moment to something which is more valuable.
—T. S. Eliot, "Tradition and the Individual Talent"

. . .

A little after noon, Mulberry Street, almost deserted, Angelo's, a long and narrow space, expensively decorated, not in the family style. They seat me toward the front, back to wall, clear view of door and street and assassins, should they decide that this is the place, this is the moment, it's you, Frank. At a front corner table, on a clean diagonal with mine, a couple has gotten here before me. Here when the place opened, maybe before (yes, before), because they have already killed half a bottle of wine, and a large antipasto is about to go too. Angelo's opens at twelve. I got there at twelve-ten. I wonder how these Chinese people got into an Italian restaurant well before opening time, in Little Italy, where the Italians have been leaving in droves, many in resentment, I hear, of an exploding Chinatown pouring over the border.

The man and the woman are probably in their early thirties, probably not married, speaking their native tongue. A waiter approaches their table and the Chinese man shifts effortlessly into Italian dialect to the waiter who, like all the waiters, is Italian-born. The Chinese man tells the waiter that he's from Calabria, born and raised, *sono di Calabria,* and the waiter says back quickly, as if picking up his cue, that one of his coworkers (whom he now calls over) is also *di Calabria.* The Chinese Calabrian and the standard Calabrian shake hands, glad to meet each other. The three men exchange pleasantries with a certain gravity of tone. The waiters depart and the Chinese man who said *sono di Calabria* turns to the woman he's with and they resume speaking in what I thought was their native tongue, intimately, with no quick over-the-shoulder glances at the waiter, no telling grins. I assume they're not talking about Calabria, but who knows.

Either this is all, on both sides, the best deadpan act known to man, or what has been said between the parties is literally true. I try hard to imagine what it would mean, what possibly, if either of my options for reading this scene were valid, and I cannot imagine it. If this is theater, who is it theater for? I check the waiters, hoping to pick up something ironical from that quarter. Nothing. They're talking about someone's son-in-law, *un cazzone proprio* (a true prick).

In his essay on Dante, Eliot says that "genuine poetry can communicate before it is understood." At Angelo's, in cognitive darkness, I sink into delight in the surfaces of whatever it is that is passing before me.

Midway through my main course: a dish of potatoes (small spheres thereof), mushrooms, onions, asparagus, artichoke hearts, zucchini, and many little excellent sausages, lucidly spiced in a light red sauce (*alto Italiano*). A couple now seated immediately to my right, a family of three to my immediate left. The woman of the couple to my right orders the fettuccine Alfredo and then asks the waiter (who is also my waiter) if the Alfredo comes with mushrooms. The waiter explains that it's the other fettuccine on the menu, in the red sauce, that has the mushrooms. The woman says that she doesn't want that one, she wants the Alfredo and she wants it with mushrooms. She's not pushy; she's nice. I have to sneak a glance over my right shoulder to get a look at her. I sneeze. She says, God bless you. I thank her, talking into my coffee.

The family of three to my left. The man has an important body: six foot two, tremendous shoulders, two hundred and seventy-five pounds, steel in the face, a belly of real force. Middle fifties. The wife, not rotund in the stereotypical manner but not slim, glasses, unconcerned. The daughter, sixteen or seventeen, petite, working on petite, unconcerned, elsewhere.

When they come in, the man sits and the wife and the daughter do not hesitate, they go straight for the ladies' room. The waiter, the one who took the Alfredo with mushrooms order and who introduced his colleague to the Chinese Calabrian, comes over to the big man, who must be a regular and who must know this waiter well, because the waiter without being asked brings him a nice antipasto and when the waiter asks, in Italian, after *la signora,* the big man answers, in Italian, "Attending to her cunt." That is what the man said. You had to be there for this part, you had to have a little Italian because the poetry is traduced by the translation (I've lost most of mine but retain the valuable words).

The man with the important body says the words wearily but with real respect. "Attending to" is my effort to get to the formal and elevated quality of his *Attenta alla sua.* The man with the important body must believe (this is what I believe) that his wife is in reality *signora* number 2, that she is attending to *signora* number 1, with whom he has a relationship, but not one that could be characterized by the elegance of *Attenta alla sua.* His relations with the two signoras appear to be tinged with the sadness of one who in the not too distant past suffered a sudden, debilitating self-appraisal and then quickly relinquished to destiny. It is perhaps no longer proper to say of the two signoras that they are "his." In the middle years of his marriage, the big man finds himself cast in a new role, by whom or what he does not know. His wife is unreadable. Nevertheless, he is to play, this he knows, *la signora* number 3. He will not complain. He will grow into the role. It will be remarked, eventually, that his performance is definitive.

Of course, the famous English monosyllable is not what he said, and cannot compare to the trochaic rhythm of the two-syllabled Italian slang term, whose spelling I am unsure of. I have never seen it written; I cannot find it in my large Italian dictionary and do not bother to look into the one for tourists. I could call Margaret Brose at the University of California, Santa Cruz, a specialist in the literature and language, but I don't know Margaret that well, haven't spoken to her in years, and do not wish to prepare the elaborate transition that would permit me to pose the overwhelming question.

I believe the second syllable of the word I could spell, because that sound ends my name: *c-c-h-i-a*. I believe that the first syllable must be spelled *m-i-n*. Thus: *mincchia*. On the other hand, I am unsure of those *c*'s. Does *mincchia,* like Lentricchia, have two *c*'s? If two *c*'s, then you must linger on the *c* in order to indicate doubleness. Which leads us to the tricky semantic issue. (Months later I call my parents. They give me contradictory responses, so I side with my father.) The word in Italian, while making the same reference as the English word, performs another communicative task which I have overheard undertaken by Italian women of my grandmother's generation and status (of the South, of the turn of the century, of poverty, amongst themselves). You would not, in English, having just been told a startling piece of news, or having just witnessed an astounding event, exclaim *Cunt!* You would not do this. But in Italian you might, some would say you must, say *Mincchia!* In such situations you are expressing your awe, registering the presence of sublimity, you are saying it with two *c*'s. The man with the important body could manage but one *c*. The *mincchia* of defeat.

(My wife, *la vera signora,* has just walked in, I'm not making this up. I tell her, without preface, that I'm writing about cunt. She replies, without preface, "What else is there?" Is it clear why some men long for important bodies? The man on my left had an important, some might even say a major body, and I pray to Our Lady of Pompeii that it gives him some consolation.)

The wife and the daughter return from their respective involvements. The waiter spreads wide his arms, but not too wide, and says, *La signora bella! La signora bella* nods subtly and the waiter says to the big man, indicating the girl, And this is your niece? The big man says, My daughter. The waiter says, I would not have believed that you had a daughter so young. (On "so young" the daughter tilts, almost imperceptibly.) The big man nods in satisfaction; he feels a little bigger, he must, because right away he complains about the bread, he wants it exchanged. I know bread. In rapid succession I had eaten four pieces, there was nothing wrong with the bread. The waiter says, Of course we shall bring you a new basket (and now the waiter moves in swiftly for the kill—he's known all along how to rank the three signoras), and he says, But of course it will be the same. The new bread arrives and the big man says, This is better (*quest'è meglio*). The waiter grins wide. Another waiter comes up from behind him, close, very close, gives him a big hug around the belly, with one arm, and says that he, the hugged one, cannot resist the bread of this place. The petite one, without asking, picks an olive off her father's plate. *La signora bella* appears oblivious, but who knows.

Am I reporting, or making this up? I don't know the answer. Is this criticism or something else? What shall I call it? The reading of a text or the making of a text? Do I need to know how much poetry, theater, and story is objectively there, at Angelo's? How much of it lies in this beholder's eye, who spends his nights and days with Western literary masters? Is someone waiting for me to say that the theater of Angelo's is marginal to the traditional interests of mainstream Western culture? The kinship of classic and ethnic cultures in the medium of myself. But what does it mean, exactly, to say "myself" when I say "myself"? If a self is a medium, is it a self?

From the point of view of literature, the drama is only one among several poetic forms. . . . Nevertheless, the drama is perhaps the most permanent, is capable of greater variation and of expressing more varied types of society, than any other.

—T. S. Eliot, "The Possibility of a Poetic Drama"

The really fine rhetoric of Shakespeare occurs in situations where a character in the play sees *himself* in a dramatic light. . . . Is not Cyrano exactly in this situation of contemplating himself as a romantic, a dramatic figure? This dramatic sense on the part of the characters themselves is rare in modern drama. . . . But in actual life, in many of those situations in actual life which we enjoy consciously and keenly, we are at times aware of ourselves in this way. . . . A very small part of acting is that which takes place on the stage! . . . [This dramatic sense] is a sense which is almost a sense of humor (for when anyone is conscious of himself as acting, something like a sense of humor is present).

—T. S. Eliot, " 'Rhetoric' and Poetic Drama"

We sit on the floor, crowded together, at the feet of Miss Beach, who does the narration and the characters in different voices. Miss Beach can read. We can't read. It's not our fault, this is first-term kindergarten. Miss Beach asks if there is a story that we would like her to tell us. Before anyone can say anything I shout out, "Jack and the Beanstalk"! Miss Beach looks at me. She looks at me like she's thinking, What's wrong with this kid? She doesn't say, Francis, I told that story yesterday. She doesn't say a word; she stares. That's how I remember my first literary experience. I remember it not directly but by remembering the bad part whose badness was bad because of how different it was from the day before, when it must have been terrific, at the feet of Miss Beach, living in literature, which I don't remember, when I must have surrendered whatever self I had to something more valuable, something alive in Miss Beach's voice.

At the moment when Miss Beach stared but could not speak, the boy wanted to jump back into yesterday's tale but could not do so unless Miss Beach relented and let herself be the way back. She did not relent. So there he was, at the edge of the storyteller's magic circle, unable to get in, who put himself outside by a request for repetition. Let's do it again, it was so good. Of course, he knew nothing of the sort. He knew nothing. He merely felt shame and, later, when he remembers, when he writes about it, some lingering frustration. He's pissed off at Miss Beach, after all these years (forty-seven, to be exact). Italian men have long memories. Be careful, Miss Beach, wherever you are.

T. S. Eliot was born with a double hernia. His mother wouldn't let him engage in the roughhouse of playground sports. He had to be trussed, down there—think about it. I, on the other hand, when I entered the eighth grade, buried Francis for good (spelled with an *i,* don't get smart). I took on Frank. I was not born with a double hernia, there was nothing wrong with me down there.

Eliot, I read, thinks that when one is an adolescent (he often says "one") one reads certain writers—he mentions Shelley—and then, he says, one grows out of these writers, one matures. I could say that Eliot was insulated by his upper-class experience. I could say that Eliot was effete, that he insults my class and ethnic experience. I could say that in my neighborhood we never heard the word "poetry," I never knew anyone who owned a book of poems, I never saw a book of poems, who the hell was Shelley, anyway, a girl? For not knowing these things we could be called insulated, but what's the point, it's not like we had a choice. And it's not like Eliot the teenager had a choice either. (But when he wrote what he wrote about what adolescents read he was an advanced adult, and for this he is responsible.) He had to read Shelley, we had to smash things on Halloween night, in our own neighborhood. We didn't know the word "faggot," but we knew what a sissy was, we had that word. Lucky for Eliot that he didn't hang out with us.

My best friend in grade school was a black kid named Nelson Brown, angular, tough, nasty elbows. We called him Nellie. I think I felt close to Nellie because, like me, he had a girl's name, only, unlike me, he didn't seem to mind, because if he did he would have been called something else, whatever Nellie wanted, who was going to argue with him? Nellie and Franny. Inseparable.

I have a cousin, a female, of course, who got me a library card when I was seven years old. You had to be seven to qualify. I was a baseball player of neighborhood note. I knew boxing, my father took me to the fights, ringside, a vantage point from which it is clear what boxing is. And there they were on the shelves of the East Utica Branch, Utica Public Library: DiMaggio, Gehrig, Ruth, Joe Louis, I got to take them home with me, to my room, close the door.

In order to get home from the library, arms full of books (I would always take out the maximum, too many to carry), I could walk through the playground, where my friends were. That was the shortest way back, a straight line between two points. Instead, I walked around the playground, putting a two-block zone between myself and my friends, whose vile hearts and minds I knew. Me unseen, arms full of books. I think I must have had a double hernia. I think I must have been trussed, down there. Nellie would have walked right through. Nellie had real balls.

Those books were like potato chips. I even tried to read them at the dinner table. My father prohibited it, of course, but he wasn't displeased. Most of my favorite writers now are poets. The ones who aren't love words and rhythms the way the best poets love words, rhythms, and the sounds of different voices. My favorite writers are aestheticians of the peculiar, virtuosos (I like that word, it's close to "virtue") like DiMaggio, Joe Louis, the Yankee Clipper, the Brown Bomber. I'm not depressed about being called the "Dirty Harry of contemporary literary theory." Now I get to walk through the playground, carrying the poems of Shelley.

And now I don't have to depend on Miss Beach in order to get inside the magic circle. I am Miss Beach. I have gone to Angelo's twice: once in the flesh, once in writing, where it is even better, where I myself can do the narration and all the voices, enhancing myself with all the bodies in the restaurant I choose to remember, filling out Franny's skinny self, getting bigger all the time. Writing as the medium of kinship.

. . . to be educated above the level of those whose social habits and tastes one has inherited may cause a division within a man which interferes with happiness.

—T. S. Eliot, *Notes Towards the Definition of Culture*

• • •

The high school classroom of Senatro D. LaBella. Senior English with the department chairman, a legend.

We have to read *Macbeth*. We can't read *Macbeth*. So what? In college we'll major in shop, in college they don't force you to read Shakespeare unless you major in English, which is out of the question. We heard that LaBella could read him, the rumor was strong. We heard that he could actually make you like it, this is what was said.

Bald, huge tortoiseshell glasses, short (which we don't notice), he enters. His baldness stuns us, we want to be bald. A face of the highest seriousness, a visage, looking hugely down upon us, bigger than it is, thanks to that great glistening dome, like one of those cardinals Raphael painted.

The man moves swiftly, if only for a few steps, erect, everything pulled together, severely graceful. His body is an edge, space is resistant stuff which he slices through as if his freedom, whose basis we would never guess, were in the balance.

We wait for the smile; we need the smile. It comes suddenly and rarely, but it comes. He had done everything, or was about to do everything—this is what the smile said—and he would do it, or had done it, with maximum sleekness.

In the halls, on the move like a cruising animal, he banters ironically with students, without distance. The athletes like him. This man was raised in Utica, in our neighborhood on Bleecker Street. He had returned to live on Bleecker Street, he drives an Olds 88 six blocks long and he speaks English as we have never heard it spoken. On Bleecker Street. No imposed tone, it's the clarity, with respect for every letter and sound of every word, and when he talks, words become things, each with its unique identity. To speak the language as he speaks it has to be an erotic experience and just hearing him teaches us that language is a thing that can be loved, that such love (it dare not speak its name in today's academy) will be requited with the favors that quench all desire. He never says that to us directly, it was unsayable in our neighborhood, but this is what he teaches. The way he talks we find funny and awesome. We love him because he is a part of us, and we love him because he isn't a part of us.

He enters, not with the class text under his arm but with a book containing all of Shakespeare, two columns, mean print, a fat, frightening thing that he holds without fear. Today we're scared because today we're supposed to discuss *Macbeth.* But we don't discuss *Macbeth,* he knows better. Instead, he reads out loud every line of the play over a period of three weeks. He does all the parts. The thing is clear, we understand the thing, we're shocked, and we feel a little noble.

The classroom of Senatro D. LaBella is set at Proctor High School, east side of Utica, approximately 1,500 students, approximately two of whom are not Italian-American Catholics whose grandparents came over (for reasons anyone in the neighborhood would understand, I count the Lebanese and the Poles with the Italian-American Catholics). We don't know Verdi or Dante (neither do the Lebanese and the Poles), we never heard of them. Most of our parents didn't get to go to high school. We didn't think of ourselves as underprivileged.

Shakespeare is a secret. LaBella tells us the secret. The secret is good but the man who tells it is better than Shakespeare because he makes it possible for us to learn new secrets on our own. He is a teacher, Senatro the Beautiful.

Most of the guys I knew at Proctor High believed he could get it every night, but that he didn't because he had other things on his mind. (I don't know what the girls thought.) The man was complex. When he taught us, we couldn't separate Shakespeare from LaBella. Shakespeare didn't exist for us except in LaBella, inside him, flowing forth on that burnished voice. It has never occurred to me that such knowledge, of Shakespeare living in the flesh and voice of my teacher, would divide me against myself and my background, that it would, in Eliot's words, "interfere with happiness." I know what Eliot is implying. No one should be able to stomach the idea.

This is what I like to imagine: it is early spring of 1958, I am sitting in LaBella's classroom during his one-man Shakespeare festival. Sitting across from me is T. S. Eliot, recently appointed Inspector of Schools for the United States. Eliot has serious theories and concerns about the relations of education and culture. He wants cultures to be organic wholes, he wants all the activities of culture to serve and express the whole, and he wants us to be, and to feel, connected to something larger than ourselves, something more valuable than our puny individual persons. Eliot believes that this state of affairs doesn't obtain, anywhere. He wants it to obtain. He refuses to admit that he's a utopian, and he thinks that the United States in particular has gone to hell.

He watches LaBella, and he watches the students watch

LaBella. I watch him. I can tell he's pleased, I can tell he wants to stay in this classroom all day. He won't, but he wants to. He thinks he needs to be someplace else.

This is also what I like to imagine: the self of the almost eighteen-year-old Frank, magically augmented by the self he would become at fifty-one, carrying a sheaf of quotations neatly copied out from Eliot's essay on Marie Lloyd, the music hall artist whose death moved Eliot to cultural mourning. When the class is adjourned, the two Franks follow Eliot out, accost him, hand him the notes. If Eliot is flustered he doesn't show it. He reads: ". . . it is not always easy to distinguish superiority from great popularity, when the two go together."

And then he reads my marginal note:

"Why would you want to, if they go together?"

And then he reads:

"And popularity in her case . . . is evidence of the extent to which she represented and expressed that part of the English nation which has perhaps the greatest vitality and interest. . . . Marie Lloyd's audiences were invariably sympathetic, and it was through this sympathy that she controlled them."

And then my note:

"His students as audience. LaBella as Marie."

And then he reads:

". . . no other comedian succeeded so well in giving expression to the life of that audience, in raising it to a kind of art. It was, I think, this capacity for expressing the soul of the people that made Marie Lloyd unique, and that made her audience . . . not so much hilarious as happy."

My note:

"I'll try to arrange coffee with you and LaBella. He has a lot on his mind, but he might consent. No promises. I could get you an apartment, cheap, in east Utica, the whole second floor of a two-family house."

He reads:

"In the music-hall comedian they find the expression and dignity of their own lives. . . ."

Me:

"No comment."

And he reads:

"The working man who went to the music-hall and saw Marie Lloyd and joined in the chorus was himself performing part of the act; he was engaged in that collaboration of the audience with the artist which is necessary in all art and most obviously in dramatic art."

Me:

"We fed him, we were part of his performance of *Macbeth*."

Eliot takes a parting shot at young Frank: "But, clearly," he says, "Shakespeare is no expression of your culture." (The emphasis is almost inaudible, but it's there, on "your.") The young Frank fears the tall smart man, but he manages this: "We know guys like Macbeth, we definitely heard of his wife." Eliot is merciless: "You attest to the power of the type to cross cultures, not to the specificity of your own." (Subtle emphasis on "own.") Young Frank doesn't follow that one. Nevertheless, he strikes back: "I heard you were from St. Louis, so how come you talk like that?" Eliot has never been asked this in his life and, stunned by the vulgar thrust, blurts it out, in a tone that might almost be described as passionate: "Because it makes me feel better, because I feel at home in it."

Eliot feels outside but he covers up very well. He leaves, returning to his home in London, the place he describes in *The Waste Land* as "Unreal City," city of the living dead.

In a few weeks I shall introduce my students in the New York program to *The Waste Land*. Can I be their Marie Lloyd? Do they want that? Do I? Will we be able to say, afterwards, We resurrected it, we saw ourselves in Eliot's world, we saw ourselves strangely, but more truly, and we cannot go back to the way we were? To sift their consciousness into the world through the medium of *The Waste Land*. I, the sifter. A good thing? Or assault with a deadly weapon?

This time through (how many times have I done this?) I am snagged yet again by a passage which by Eliot's standards is plain and, out of context, even easy. The passage is shocking for its positive charge, its warm tone, its longing for the actual. It doesn't belong to *The Waste Land* that we have long known. Our guide through the desert of the contemporary, the poem's voice-over, the authoritative voice that opens the poem ("April is the cruellest month") and that reappears frequently in judgment, covert and dour, just as frequently (despite its desire to stay outside) falls inside, becoming itself a subject of waste. This walker in the city suddenly sounds almost happy. This moment, this place seem almost to suffice. I can't find any other passage in the poem remotely resembling this one. I check the work of the Eliot experts, who have been so helpful in clearing up allusive obscurities. They note that the first line is a quotation from *The Tempest,* but this I knew. Such plainness, such absence of allusive obscurity, does not require their explicating finesse. How does the passage work with the rest of the poem? Why has this passage fascinated me for so long?

> *'This music crept by me upon the waters'*
> *And along the Strand, up Queen Victoria Street.*
> *O City city, I can sometimes hear*
> *Beside a public bar in Lower Thames Street,*
> *The pleasant whining of a mandoline*
> *And a clatter and a chatter from within*
> *Where fishmen lounge at noon: where the walls*
> *Of Magnus Martyr hold*
> *Inexplicable splendour of Ionian white and gold.*

Another fragment, cut off from what comes before and after by extra spacing. The quotation from *The Tempest:* a line spoken by Ferdinand, part of a complete sentence formed by Eliot's first two lines. One sentence, two voices (*The Waste Land:* one poem, countless voices). Eliot assumes the mask of Ferdinand-in-mourning, who has just lost his father and friends in a storm at sea (so he thinks), and is now being led by strange music (Ariel's song) to this bank, on this island ("Weeping again the king my father's wrack"), the music allaying his passion as well as the storm. In a moment, just a few lines later, Ferdinand will meet Miranda and fall instantly in love, and eventually all will be well.

The music that Eliot's waste land guide hears as he stands outside a public bar is equally alluring. The sounds of conversation and the other sounds that float out to him from the inside must please him as much as the music of the pleasant mandoline (note the amusing internal rhyme, "clatter" and "chatter"). The mandoline of the new Ariel draws him to the pub. This is his destination, but not his destiny. He does not go in. How come?

And there is a third Ferdinand, this one drawn by the Ariel music that Eliot himself makes in writing this passage as a lyric surge, all the more alluring for being one of the rare lyric surges of the poem. The third Ferdinand: I, the reader. The pub, the fishmen (not fishermen, these are workers from a nearby fishmarket), the fishmen who "lounge," the pleasant mandoline (from *mandolino,* an Italian word): the pub as Prospero's island in the waste land of the great modern city. The poetry itself, the lyric surge itself, as Prospero's island in *The Waste Land*. The streets are specified. This is the route of a magical journey whose end does not turn out well for Eliot.

From Bleecker and Carmine to Sixth Avenue, south to Broome, east to Mulberry, south onto Mulberry, left-hand side of the street: 146. I went in. Angelo's restaurant as Prospero's island. How does it turn out for me?

Eliot looks at the contemporary world through a Shakespearean lens, and by so doing tells us that he is bereft, like Ferdinand; tells us that he wants it to turn out well, as it did for Ferdinand. In this poem of numerous failures of love, is Eliot telling us that he wants to meet Miranda? Eliot sees the scene, or tries to see the scene, as an episode of romance drama. But at the same time he cherishes the scene for what it is. He gives the names of things, the scene holds its own ground. Eliot is decent to his materials. Shakespeare and *il mandolino* in harmony, the two cultures not at war.

From the pub to Magnus Martyr, adjacent places, shifting attention. The pub and Magnus Martyr are companionable expressions of a unified culture. Eliot doesn't go in, he doesn't belong, though he needs to belong. He needs to be able to move effortlessly, naturally, between pub and church, without thinking. The "inexplicable splendour": this is good, not to have to explain, splendor is not for explaining. He may write in fragments but he doesn't want to live that way. He wants to live in a culture organically whole. Maybe the point about the mandoline episode is that it doesn't fit, as an alternative vision is not supposed to fit.

I could weave Angelo's into the seminar, easily, but it might be a mistake. They might say, You went in, ethnic Frank, Eliot didn't. They might say, You have an inside relation to the ethnic pleasures of the Angelo's text. They might say, You are a privileged reader of the Angelo's text. And then we would all sing the multicultural rag. Better to tell them you were a transparency at Angelo's. Tell them you didn't want to be noticed, that you wanted to disappear into all that you beheld. Tell them you weren't a contributing actor at the Theater of Angelo's. That you want to belong, but you don't belong. Tell them not to use you to beat up on Eliot. Tell them that your wife is not an Italian-American, and she has written the two best Italian-American short stories you've ever read. No, I am not Marie Lloyd, nor was meant to be.

I could, but I don't live on the second floor of a two-family house in east Utica. I left Utica for good in 1966.

. . .

Having sacrificed yourself to something more valuable, in the text of Angelo's, or in the formal text of a poem, you are tempted to move above, in an effort to explain why you tell the stories you tell about men with important bodies, Miss Beach, Senatro the Beautiful, or some of the *Cantos* of Ezra Pound, which you are reading with your students in the Duke in New York program, hoping to teach them that the *Cantos* are about reading as a medium of kinship. Having yielded, having taken a vacation from who you are, having in a way forgotten yourself in order to find a more satisfying self, you begin to reflect on your "position" and "allegiances." You want to announce principles of literary criticism. You would propound a theory. You've been having a good time, but now, should you yield to the Devil, you're going to have a very bad time. So bad, should you yield, that you'll tell yourself that you made a serious mistake when almost thirty years ago you decided you wanted to teach literature and write about it.

You want to resist, and you do resist by remembering three passages in written texts that have given pleasure. You tell yourself that you are not evading the task that Mark Edmundson offered and which you accepted. You tell yourself that what you remember will silence the Devil for good, who wants you to become abstract, because abstraction is the stuff of his kingdom. The Devil of Theory: you know him well.

The first passage, from Ralph Waldo Emerson, has for years attracted and repulsed you: "Standing on the bare ground—my head bathed by the blithe air, and uplifted into infinite space—all mean egotism vanishes. I become a transparent eyeball. I am nothing. I see all. The currents of the Universal Being circulate through me; I am part or parcel of God. The name of the nearest friend sounds then foreign and accidental: to be brothers, to be acquaintances, master or servant is then a trifle and a disturbance." You like the phrase "I become a transparent eyeball. I am nothing," because it reminds you of what happens to you in Angelo's, and on Seventh Avenue, and at Coole Park, and when reading Wallace Stevens, and in that monastery that you visited almost six months ago. Different places. You like the distinction implied by "mean egotism," because you know that some capacity for selfhood and ego must remain, some capacity for reception, that which receives and registers the pleasure of seeing all. The "I" that "sees all" is still an "I," but a different kind of "I." You don't know what "the Universal Being" means, especially with capital letters, and you don't care. You suspect Emerson is saying that he feels good, and that this is his way of putting it. The last sentence, "The name of the nearest friend sounds then foreign and accidental," you don't like at all and you wonder why Emerson didn't go all the way and say "dearest friend." Maybe not even Emerson in that mood could bring himself to such iciness, so he changed *d* to *n*. In the last sentence, Emerson sees nothing at all. But you will always read Emerson because the conflict in the famous "transparent eyeball" passage is staged again and again in his work, and you can think of no conflict more basic, and not just to writers and readers.

The second passage is from Thomas Merton's autobiography, *The Seven Storey Mountain,* which you are now reading, though you promised yourself you would never read it. You are gripped as you are rarely gripped by the pages on his decision to enter Our Lady of Gethsemani, in Kentucky, and especially by the pages that describe the moments of entry. Then you read this passage: "I was free. I had recovered my liberty. I belonged to God, not to myself: and to belong to Him is to be free, free of all the anxieties and worries and sorrows that belong to this earth, and the love of things that are in it. What was the difference between one place and another, one habit and another, if your life belonged to God, and if you placed yourself completely in His hands? The only thing that mattered was the fact of the sacrifice, the essential dedication of one's self, one's will. The rest was only accidental." You like the sentence "I belonged to God, not to myself," you understand that he had sacrificed himself to something more valuable (Merton admired Eliot, too), but the rest of the passage causes you to think that if belonging to God entails *that,* then to hell with God. You appreciate, however, the situation whose recollection must have produced those sentences and sentiments, and you know how much the rest of Merton's life will be a repudiation of those sentences and sentiments, how much he will suffer the pains and pleasures of being in place, how much he will cherish the so-called accidents of distinction in persons, things, and places.

The sentence in Merton about what was the difference between one place and another rings a bell. You search through Don DeLillo's *Ratner's Star* and you find this, in about ten seconds: " 'What is this but a place?' he said. 'Nothing more than a place. We're both here in this place, occupying space. Everything is a place. All places share this quality. Is there any real difference between going to a gorgeous mountain resort with beautiful high thin waterfalls so delicate and ribbonlike that they don't even splash when they hit bottom—waterfalls that *plash,* is this so different from sitting in a kitchen with bumpy linoleum and grease on the wall behind the stove across the street from a gravel pit? What are we talking about? Two places, that's all. There's nowhere you can go that isn't a place. So what's such a difference? If you can understand this idea, you'll never be unhappy.' " DeLillo tells us that in Ratner's voice (it is Ratner himself who is speaking) there remains only the trace of Brooklyn's "desperate melodies." The man rushes madly into abstraction, but DeLillo lets us hear the traces, this is a Brooklyn Jew, this famous Nobel Laureate, not just anybody, and we hear the music in "So what's such a difference?" You're glad that DeLillo saves Ratner from himself by giving him those long and funny descriptions of place difference which dominate his theme of place sameness. You like that.

PART
TWO

In the Cage

November 1991–April 1992

4

Have you practis'd so long to learn to read?
Have you felt so proud to get at the meaning of poems?
　　　　　　—WALT WHITMAN, "SONG OF MYSELF"

I think we are in rats' alley . . .
　　　　　　—T. S. ELIOT, *THE WASTE LAND*

I loved the heat of New York in August, when I took to the streets of lower Manhattan and greeted the horrors of the alphabet avenues. In August, when New Yorkers want to be elsewhere, I wanted to be here, and I just barely walked: I sailed, cruised, became everything that I saw, and I liked what I became. Me and my fierce joy and the scenes of lower Manhattan, what was the difference?

But then I finished the piece on my kinsman, T. S. Eliot, then the weather turned cold in November and it was difficult to smell the bracing urine. The molecules started crowding together, the thousand pieces of my happy scattered self gathered and congealed, my students became bored (they said they were "intimidated," I must look like a maniac). The writing dried up. I walked less, slept more, hope in the morning, naps in the afternoon (then naps in the morning too), and I returned to myself, and I was nothing that I saw. And then it started to come on, it arrived, there it was: my bonnie lass, Rage, my salvation. *Smash a face into the sidewalk, any face, blend it right in, face-flesh concrete, something new in the world, like a poem, this smashing moment, like living in a poem.*

"Tell them you didn't want to be noticed, that you wanted to become all that you beheld." "Tell them you didn't want to be noticed, that you wanted to disappear into all that you beheld." Two versions of a sentence that I am trying to get right, at the end of my meditation on my kinsman, T. S. Eliot. Which is better? Which tells the truth of my desire? Become or disappear? Revising a sentence, hung between being who I am (and what is that?) and two versions of the promised end, two kinds of nothingness—in imagination, both pleasurable. Last revision: the way back to the writing that was, the writing of my self-forgetfulness, and the ease of my life in those easy sentences.

In autumn's advancing cold, I wrote words in my little red notebook: "werewolf," "vampire," "Jekyll and Hyde," "Rumpelstiltskin." I wrote the most hopeful sentence that I have ever written in my little red notebook, which I keep on my bedside table, to look at late, to thumb through, to have and to hold, to love and to cherish, before I turn out the lights. I copy the sentence out now in the belief (why do I believe this?) that the act of copying will commit me to the act presaged in my hopeful sentence, which says: "I returned to Mepkin Abbey in order to be exorcised."

In the autumn, I read, for the first time, Bram Stoker's *Dracula,* from which I learned a new word, which I copy into my little red notebook: "zoophagous" (life-eating). "Metamorphosis and murder—themes of the werewolf." I thought I wrote that too in my little red notebook, but I can't find it now. Did I read those words somewhere or do I want to read those words, then do those words? How much do werewolves remember of what they have done after they change back? Let us pray.

It arrives, there it is, it's me.

I found myself (I must try harder not to say "myself") in the autumn, in the advancing cold, sucked back into the corpse of my everyday life, the corpse who am. What sucked me back in? The condition of nonwriting? But now the words come, now the ice melts, now I flow forth, I come fully forward, into the room, where I rarely am, even when I am in the room, "in body." *(Yes, that is his body, that is the body of Frank Lentricchia. Frank himself is not here.)* People are getting to know me. *Hello, Frank. My God! Frank! How you've changed!* So much the better to eat you, my dear.

And I've become the athlete of the incredible. Lucky, when it comes on, that there is gravity, or I'd spring too far, off the face of the earth. Rumpelstiltskin stomps through the floor in a heaviness, a downward perfection of rage. I become the quintessence of lightness, the world record for the pole vault falls, Look Ma! without a pole, without even a running start, my vaulting, my bonnie Rage. I, the transcendental Rumpelstiltskin. When I return to the earth, my heel into its face.

In the unexpurgated text of the Brothers Grimm, Rumpelstiltskin, in the lyricism of rage, tears himself in half. Frank is not my real name, can you guess my real name? Do you have a thing for my bonnie lass? Shall we be kin, and less than kind?

When I left the protective confines of my Italian-American fortress on the east side of Utica, they used to ask me, How do you pronounce your name? What kind of a name is that? Are you Polish? Imagine having a name like Rumpelstiltskin; imagine the questions. I think that they forced him to take his name underground (you will find none of this in the Brothers Grimm), that was the true beginning, when they forced him to look at it, he had never done that, he feared he'd become his name, that's when it started to come on.

And would it have been different, do you think, if the name had been George Gordon, Lord Byron, or Greta Garbo, or Joe DiMaggio? The name is always ugly, when it's yours, and you didn't make it up.

They found out, they always do. So he tore himself in half: not in rage but in cleverness. He would give them half, they could call it Rumpelstiltskin. The other half would be free, his no–name-self. The thing about spinning gold out of straw was a ruse to keep them off the track. For a while, it worked. They could have the gold and the queen's beautiful child, he didn't give a shit, the beautiful child wasn't the point.

You want to know the point? A reasonable desire. The desire of reason itself: to know the point. To explain rage. But the name does not explain. None of the circumstances of rage explain. It stands apart, anterior, the rage itself: waiting. To explain rage? Like Victor Frankenstein (how would you like to have that name?) trying to discover and harness the principle of life. The queen's beautiful child does not explain because nothing explains rage's finest moment, the radically creative burst which brings into the world a nameless self, torn free from the man who used to be. (Who said men can't give birth?) Stop this day and night with me and I will show you the point.

I live in the literary academy, the Imperial Palace of Explanation, among those-who-always-already-know, among the Princes and Princesses of Pre-Reading, the executioners of mystery.

In the absence of knowing, perhaps a very great good.

"How would you describe it?"
"As the achievement of intimacy. The ice melts."
"You like it?"
"Yes."
"When you vent it on the innocent, you like that?"

"Yes."

"As much as when you vent it on the guilty?"

"No difference, when I vent it."

"You cannot tell the difference?"

"You deaf?"

"But afterwards, the distinction is known to you?"

"Yes."

"And how do you feel afterwards, about the innocent?"

"Guilty. But not right away."

"I do not mean to imply that you should vent it on the guilty. Not even the guilty deserve what you vent."

"Of course."

"But will you vent it again upon the innocent?"

"Of course."

"On the innocent?"

"You deaf?"

"You know that they are innocent before, and after, but during you do not know?"

"During is a pleasure. During is during."

(pause)

"During is during."

"Yes."

(pause)

"But what do you intend to do, for the future, in order to protect the innocent?"

"Nothing."

"I cannot accept that, I cannot accept nothing."

"You want something to accept?"

. . .

I'm not supposed to be writing this, I'm supposed to be finishing my never-ending book on modernism, the last chapter, the others have been done for so long (I almost wrote "dead for so long"). I'm supposed to be writing on T. S. Eliot. (But I have said this before.) Everything in the poetry, the magical poetry, resists what I say about it.

Midnight, I cannot sleep, and I reread *The Waste Land* in a virgin edition, untouched by my marginalia, all my glosses on all those sources and allusions, no mystery to me ever since I was an undergraduate, thirty years ago, but which, nevertheless, I gloss again and again, year in and year out, in nice new clean editions, the little paperback, writing out the notes, the ones I already know.

I cannot bear to read my many older editions, do not wish to touch them, with my notes written in, the ones I already know. Revolting to gaze at my handwriting, changing crazily every year. The notes themselves invariably neat and legible. It's the style of the hand, that's it. Best to say "the hands," more honest. As in: "an anthology of essays, by several hands." The hand is foreign, somebody else's, always.

What might the handwriting experts say when they arrive to examine the relevant documents ("draped by the beneficent spider") in my empty room? This is what they will say: "Notice the style of the *e* in 1975. No evidence of that manifestation before or since. Observe the elongated lettering and leftward slant of 1979. Changed utterly in 1980. It appears that he could not control his hand. It seems an extravagance to say 'he,' a metaphysical leap in the dark. We have here, in these specimens of his hand, the excrement of a personality in fragments, evidence of a case of total possession.

The coroner's report may supply us with the corroboration we neither seek nor refuse. Were there, in fact, two small perforations on the throat, along the line of the jugular, consistent with the possibility of the canine incisors? Gentlemen: For many years, Frank Lentricchia may not, as such, have existed."

Maybe this time. November 1991. I'll fashion a hand for the clean hardcover of Eliot's complete poems, the New York edition, a hand that will happily endure, that I will recognize, warmly, in an assurance, a pleasure of intimate persistence. The "intensest rendezvous." To make myself, once and for all.

I glance at them from time to time, these old editions, carried without pleasure to New York, so hard to avoid on the bookshelves in this elegant loft, on my second honeymoon, a new start, in New York. I do not wish to write in this virgin hardcover, but I must. This time in fine light pencil, definitively, notes in the hand's definitive style, my self revealed, critical apocalypse, the text revealed, the future mastered, throw away the old editions, destroy the evidence. A presence of selfhood, self-mastering self, here in this elegant loft, here on Fifteenth and Seventh, in this city, O City.

Midnight. I take the poem. *The Waste Land* in one sweeping glance, one breath, performing it for my mind's ear, with fierce joy, like an extended aria marked *legato,* imagining myself a virtuoso tenor of criticism, in the *bel canto* style. I cannot fall asleep, and in the dark I luxuriate in my performance, standing ovations, shouts of *Encore!*

And all night long, the other, nonperforming "I" rehearses words about the magic of the poetry and the magic of the performance—how shall I separate them?—but my words are no good, the words about the magic do not communicate the magic, my words about the magic are dull. Only the magic can communicate the magic.

Dull words rattle, through the autumn they hound me, in my brain. Violence. He should be the one done violence by my words, but it's me. I can't hurt him. He escapes, as always.

My students find us both dull. I cannot control my hand. The magic exceeds my words about the magic. I think it exceeds the poetry. Something in me is exceeding everything.

Here she comes, my bonnie lass, coming through the rye, my bonnie Rage, mad to see her man. Would my bonnie reader like a piece? How about a *ménage à trois*? Did you not tell me that your sentences were coming much too slowly?

T. S. Eliot is dead. May my dull words keep him dead.

"You want to go out the fucking window?"
(silence)
"How about the Brooklyn Bridge? Yes or no?"
(silence)
"You look nice."
(silence)
"You fucking deaf?"
(silence)
"Have I told you? Have I told you lately how much I love you?"
(silence)

• • •

His physical health is deteriorating, his mental health is even worse (I'm not talking about myself, it's Eliot, I'm back at Eliot). He works too much (Eliot, not me): the bank, teaching, editing, writing. His wife is ill, constantly, and not just in body. His marriage is a madhouse. He is the author of a famous poem, "The Love Song of J. Alfred Prufrock," it is 1919, and he writes an essay, "Hamlet and His Problems," in which he calls Shakespeare's play "the 'Mona Lisa' of litera- ture." He says that it is "most certainly an artistic failure." He's thirty-one years old and this is how he talks: ". . . most certainly an artistic failure." The essay should be called "El- iot and His Problems." A couple of years later he publishes *The Waste Land,* which also should be called "Eliot and His Problems." And what should this writing be called? Do not tell me.

T. S. Eliot the essayist speaks often with stiff, pontifical solemnity. Those are his words of self-characterization, but he never changed the tone and style of his voice. I'm wagering that the style of his hand never wavered. He is all reason, he is The Man Who Knows. But *Hamlet* knocks him off his throne. It resists. He cannot explain. He finds himself speak- ing in contradictions, his reason is undone, but he covers up brilliantly with that voice of his, so full of confidence.

Hamlet, "most certainly an artistic failure," is "puzzling and disquieting," he says, more so than any other of Shake- speare's plays, and "profoundly interesting," he says, more so than *Coriolanus* and *Antony and Cleopatra,* which are Shake- speare's "most assured" artistic successes, but which are not (he admits this) as "profoundly interesting" as *Hamlet.*

Eliot decides that in *Hamlet* Shakespeare was dealing

with "intractable material," material that will not take the impress of motive. Whatever it is that moves his title character cannot be brought home to language, dramatic situation, all the circumstances of character. A motive unspeakable. It is the motive that is "intractable" (this is mine, my point, not Eliot's).

Interesting word, "intractable": not easily governed or tamed (obstinate, refractory), as in "an intractable temper"; not easily manipulated or wrought; not easily relieved or cured, as in "an intractable malady." Sounds good. Sounds like, if you have to have a self, that's what you want it to be: "intractable," as in "can't be fucked with." That's what you want: an incurable malady of self, if you have to have a self.

Something in Hamlet is exceeding everything. This is what I believe. I wonder what Hamlet would have done if T. S. Eliot had said to him, Your feelings are too much, they are in excess of your situation. I know what I would do, and I think that my bonnie reader knows too.

5

Now, in midwinter, when my older daughter, her name is Amy (meaning, in French, the loved one, but the name does not ward off the evil of love withheld), when her call wakes me in the middle of the night—the next morning I am to return to Mepkin Abbey—her voice pitched up and distorted, "Dad, something happened," I respond with the right words (I said the right thing), not from form, but were they words of the heart?, my voice pitched up and distorted (I am too far away to help, I am not there), and the conversation is concluded, and the right thing has been said, was it from the heart? (the rightness of the words my wife's judgment), I am a cliché, the divorced father who wasn't there.

What did I have, when I hung up the phone, in the middle of the night, besides memory of words whose heart-feltness I do not recall, not now, not even when I hung up the phone? This corpse, this is what I have, this self, this son I never had. I did not cancel my trip to the monastery.

And it will not give solace, not in the middle of the night, to reenact the role of the god whose only need is to dole out punishment to his all-sufficient Self. Himself over Himself. That's a stratagem for the middle of the day, your gift to intimates, privileged to sit as audience in the theater of yourself, in order to watch you play your signature role; who are granted opportunity to salve your wounds; who will give (freely, they believe) what your performance cunningly elic-its, the wished-for response: *Frank, you're too hard on yourself.* And there's the rub, the hypocrisy of your much-flourished autonomy (from the Greek *hypokritēs,* signifying "actor on the stage"). Take a bow, scrupulous narcissist.

You were dwelling, were you not, on your daughter, dwelling with her in thought, but with whom do you dwell now in your comforting little meditator's room at Mepkin Abbey? You love the mirrored barriers which confessional writing erects about you, the pleasures of solitude, scribbling notes on yourself. Admit it. Are you confessing or are you acting? Say you do not know the difference: make your true confession. Where shall your sincerity be located, in this thea-ter of yourself? Will there be no end to this duplicity? Who speaks? Who says, Will there be no end to this duplicity?

Who desires sincerity? Tell us, what have you given? Speak, preening self-dramatist.

Invoke the God of Keys, hear Him turn the key, then the clicking of the lock, the swinging open of the door, and the unscrewing of the door from the doorjambs.

It's 4:30 A.M., Brother Christian is celebrating the mass. Brother Christian is seventy-eight years old, but his voice is not. We've reached the place of the saying of the prayers of intercession. There are three retreatants: two nuns, of the Little Sisters of Jesus, who stand next to me, so much the better to help me find my way through the texts, and whose ruddy health is attractive, and is distracting me. And me, specialist in the pale cast of thought, with a bad cold. Brother Christian delivers the last prayer. He speaks: "For university professors: that they may communicate true values in their teaching, and by the example of their lives."

"Dad, I'm calling at this incredible hour, don't be mad, Dad, because I can't hold it in any longer. Guess what? I just finished the last revisions of my secret book. It's all about you! I'm totally fair from my own point of view. Guess what? Harcourt Brace Jovanovich will publish it in six months. You know, the company that's not interested in your work. Dad, we're writers together at last, we're two of a kind."

She dropped something heavy on her bare foot; I can't remember what it was. A kitchen accident. How bad a sign is it that I can't remember? I remember Beckett: "Can there be misery—loftier than mine? No doubt." I never asked what she was doing in her kitchen in the middle of the night, why weren't you in bed, Amy, where you belonged? Where normal people are at that hour. How come? I want an answer now, goddamn it. I never said that to my twenty-year-old daughter, who's living on her own. She broke her big toe, I forget which foot, my memory's normally excellent, and she had to go to the Emergency Room. I didn't tell her that the anxiety and terror in her voice were too big for the facts of her case. I didn't tell her that my anxiety and terror were not reduced, not by an iota, by my knowledge of the facts of her case. In fact, we don't know what her case is. What our case is, that's better. I remember the jet-black kitten, my gift to her, I remember his elegance, long-legged and sharp, a birthday present, her first pet. Two weeks later, she found him, stiff as a board. I have a paranoid theory about that; I like my paranoid theory. How old was she then? Maybe four or five, I can't remember. I never saw the electric beaters, mixing up a delicious cake recipe, whirring nicely along, smooth and strong, and she leans over, and she leans in, my long-haired daughter, oh delicious sweet batter, half the hair on her head ripped out of her scalp. Kitchen accidents. How old was she then? Maybe five or six. I was on the opposite coast when the call came, the divorced father who wasn't there, the teacher, visiting family in Utica, eating like four men delicious home-made calzone, the specialty of my godmother, the beautiful Rose DeCrisci, who made it for me, for Christmas. Rip my hair out, *Cumara* Rose, do it, on the left side, I see her left side, ripped out in the kitchen. Delicious sweet hair, a family recipe.

This is what I know, that what happens to my children by accident is a hint of the unspeakable. What happens by intention. This is my knowledge. Am I crazy, Amy? Get thee to a monastery, Daddy. Am I crazy? We're two of a kind, Dad, we're kitchen accidents, we're kitchen writers.

The sounds of our voices at the beginning of that phone call don't compute, this is our case, voices without adequate referent, inarticulate, birthing rage. We know this, but the knowing does not give relief, and that's another fact. God only knows, we don't add up, God knows. He knows. He knows everything. The Omnipotent Father. Son of a bitch, smug, with His Son up there on the cross, and He the Father Omniscient knowing it will turn out well. If God the Father is my father, what kind of a father is He that He won't let me the father save my daughter from her pain? How will her story turn out? I'm in the dark. He knows? He knows that accidents are intentions not yet found out, that's what He knows. He knows the names and addresses of the perpetrators. I want the names and addresses of the perpetrators, now, goddamn it. Yes, Brother Christian, by the example of my life, by my stupid impotent rage. In the absence of an appropriate object for my vengeance, I'll go after the reader, I'll show no mercy, like God my Absent Father.

To the Emergency Room, mad-Dad, get thee to the Emergency Room. He knows, Dad, He knows your name and address.

INSCRIPTION FOR A TOMBSTONE

HERE LIES THE MAN OF PRECISIONS

A PUNCTUAL MAN

UNHINGED

A SELF DECEIVED

OUR LADY OF MEPKIN

PRAY FOR HIM

NOW, IN MIDWINTER

6

And of the Cannibals that each other eat,
The Anthropophagi, and men whose heads
Do grow beneath their shoulders. This to hear
Would Desdemona seriously incline; . . . —OTHELLO, I, III

Now in April, I imagine a friend, a friendly reader, not that far away, but far enough, in a distracted state watching CNN, brooding, inaccessible, and catching a reference to a couple of gruesome murders, chunks of stinking meat and hundreds of bone fragments, this time discovered just a nice walk from our lovely home in Hillsborough, North Carolina. But he doesn't catch the name of the apprehended killer, which they're going to have trouble pronouncing and spelling down here. I, with a name they have trouble pronouncing and spelling everywhere, write to my friend, my friendly reader, and say: I didn't lure people into our lovely home (where you visited, you dined, you survived), then mutilate those poor people, have sex with their dead bodies, extract, like precious stones, their inner organs and genitalia, have sex again, this time with the severed genitalia (that I never did), force the totally liberated genitalia to have sex with each other, regardless of sexual preference, then place in our fridge, snuggled in Saran Wrap, all the delectables: livers, hearts, vaginas, penises, and kidneys (which lend to the palate "a fine tang of faintly scented urine"), then throw the rest of the shit to the fucking dog (you know damn well we don't have a fucking dog), burn what the dog and the raccoons and the possums and I can't eat with relish.

"Leopold Bloom ate with relish the inner organs of beasts and fowls." But not of humans; James Joyce loved Leopold Bloom. It wasn't me. You know it couldn't have been me. How could it have been me? I've read Joyce; I love Joyce.

I wonder what they're holding back. Not the enemies (we know what the enemies think), but the readers of clear-eyed concern, who probably already imagine what I half-hope they would never imagine, though they would never say it, being too decent to say it, but they imagine it nevertheless, because I permit them to: I, the friend who finds pleasure by writing violence, it's so easy, half-hoping to stimulate the latent voyeur in a select few—flashing exposure, then the closing of the door. How long can the readers of clear-eyed concern carry on, without letting on? What words are they trying not to say in their minds? Do they intend to spare me forever their knowledge of my crimes? Voyeurs, friendly readers, my kin—your burden of friendship is playing dumb. Mine is to pull you out of your brooding.

Flowering judas, dogwood, and azaleas. "To be eaten," now in depraved April.

PART THREE

The Glamour of Evil

May–July 1992

7

The only emperor is the emperor of ice-cream.

—WALLACE STEVENS

I'm writing again in Ireland, again in May, happily, imagining my kids reading this thing of mine. Maybe I want them to exonerate me. Curious vehicle of exoneration: my writing. At the time, when I left a five-and-a-half-year marriage that was dead from the start—in February of 1973— my kids were two and six months respectively. *("Dead from the start"? Are you writing soap opera again?)* When they were fourteen and a half and thirteen, Amy and Rachel left California to come and live with us in North Carolina.

The subject is family, and the family in question is not happy. If the subject could speak for itself (but inside the writing only the writer can speak), it might say that the happy

Italian-American writer was covering up while claiming to do the opposite, that it is not right for the writer to take pleasure in this writing, even as I do now, given the subject's experience of the writer, of which the writer is by no means ignorant. The writer's subject (his family) might conclude that it was being turned into an autobiographical fiction, that it provided the writer with just another occasion for the pleasures of composition. *(Are you putting thoughts in their heads? Trying to crawl in?)* In the coded lingo of the CIA, "the subject" is the target of assassination, and I strongly suspect that my subject has long known itself as "the subject." Composition, I mean composing, even as a form of domestic violence, is so composing. I imagine my kids talking to me about what they have read.

The monastery, they say, since when are you religious? You worrying about your age? Then you went again, no more religious the second time than the first, and you threw out the hint that maybe you shouldn't come back, you wrote out your fantasies of all of us in the family, and you added in your friends, too—do you have any?—everyone you know outside the monastery, "the unavoidables," you called us, dead. Then you evened it up by burying yourself there in that place of old men, older even than you. You talk worse than a Jewish mother.

Monastery: from the Greek, meaning hermit's cell. Monk: a man who does not, must not, take a wife, childless. Who stays out of the kitchen. Monastery and mononucleosis. Monk and monomaniac. Better spell Frank in Irish: "Frunc," courtesy of someone else's child, Simon Feeney, age eight, of Dublin, who made it up. An expert told me, Simon, it's not Irish. Frunc the Moniac. "Moniac" is mine, Simon.

At your age you want us to believe you're still carrying a grudge against your kindergarten teacher. You just love Mafia talk, it turns you on. I'm going to put out a contract on that old bitch. Just quoting the Don of Hillsborough. You like it when we say "the Don," that's why we say it. *But why represent them with a single voice? We, there is no we, they don't speak to each other.*

We knew about the manuscript in the refrigerator, we knew you did it, we've known for years, we saw it in there with our own eyes, when we were young and impressionable, *eight and six and a half, visiting one weekend,* having to see that thing in there, but we passed no judgment, we forgave you. Now it's genitalia in the refrigerator, both sexes, the cannibal without prejudice. Your manuscripts and body parts. Are they supposed to be related, or what? You want people to think you're capable of this sickness, is that it? We know who you are. We remember the monster acts you used to do when we were little, mainly for your own pleasure. Dad, what is the point of this writing? Is this your new monster act? Who are you trying to scare now? *You persist, this we, this bullshit: one of them doesn't speak to you.*

Too many extremes, that's what's hard on us, you're either a talking machine and a lot of crazy jokes, which we liked, or it's nothing, your eyes puffed up like you were in a fight, like De Niro, your man, in *Raging Bull,* your movie. A few extremes, maybe eight or nine, we could have handled. Dad, you threatened T. S. Eliot, who's dead, with severe bodily harm. What is that supposed to mean? Don't answer. *(Monk, monotone, monstrous.)* And we notice (not that we care) that you're using words in public print (this is new with you) that if we use them in private, in front of you, you give us a little cringe. *Give them harsher voices. Can you give them voices of their own?* We definitely notice that. You don't realize we notice the cringe but we notice the cringe, which you god-damn well could totally hide if you wanted to, if you exercised a little self-restraint. Has anyone ever talked to you about self-restraint? Do you even know how to spell self-restraint? No wonder why you don't want to have a self, you have too much. Consider distributing a little self to the un-avoidables. Incorporate yourself, become the East Coast distributor.

You know, when it suits you, you come on like a wop right off the boat. You're proud of this, to put it mildly. It's like a weapon, like a knife, your ethnicity. Why did you take relish in teaching us those words when we were young? Wop, greaseball, dago, guinea, spaghetti bender. You like those words, but they just bore us. We don't care.

How does it feel to get monologued? We could go on for a long time. Granted, not as long as you. Your grievances are longer, we grant it. We make no excuses for our mother. What are you going to do? Kill our mother? You better kill everybody. Go ahead, make up your mind, because you're going to do it anyway.

Now we're going to tell you something, you're the type of person, listen for a change, this is your secret, you're the type who takes pride in what a lot of people you know would take as a total insult, something you like to pass on to your so-called close friends, not to us, but we heard about it. People could never guess from the way you talk, if they didn't already know (this is you, now, bragging) that you're educated in literature, or even educated as much as you are, or even educated at all. You sound dumb. You claim someone said that to you. This is your claim. You showed us all those Scorsese movies because you want to tell us this is who you are, but this is not who you are because you read books all the time. Remember that joke you told us? Better to have books than to have children. We actually thought that was funny. Still do. Hope you do too. You're not the Don, Dad, you're the nerd of Little Italy. Frank the dumb thug. We give you the Academy Award. We think you made that story up.

And that other story, how many times are you going to tell that other story? Are you going to write about that one too? Number one on your hit parade, about how you worked, at fourteen (you emphasize fourteen) in the slaughterhouse (and you never say *a* slaughterhouse, it's always *the*). Are these stories supposed to be put-downs of your university friends? We get the point. You're not a wimp. They're all spoiled WASPs, born with silver spoons shoved up their asses. We're quoting the big poetry lover. Raging pasta. *That's not harsh, that's cute, you want them to be cute. They're past twenty. Gone from your home. Can't you give them voices of their own? Nail their voices to the page.*

But when you were clear (we'll spare you, we'll keep it in the past) you were very, very clear, and we all should have run away. You rarely talked in the house, if talk's the right word, what a joke, what you did at home (we're keeping it in the past) is not what normal people call talk. We couldn't recognize your face. You did to us what you couldn't do to our mother. You carved us up. The anger couldn't have been about what it was about, because it was too big to match anything, we knew that, but knowing that never made it any easier. *Correlated with nothing, exceeding everything, a tone, a style, a way of being in the home, among family and friends.* You filled up the room, you left us no room, a little apathy would do you some good. Any time, out of the blue, do you remember the time when the senior female in the house left the coffeepot plugged in all day? The day one of the junior females spilled soda on the precious living room rug? Do you remember? *(It was Rachel.)* Dad, we got exhausted, that's all it was, exhaustion, then we got apathetic, the apathy came on and it was good for us.

The senior female in the house, who we think could use a little apathy, your chief defender, the stepmother who defied the category *(that's not how they talk)* said it wasn't what it seemed, that's what she always said. We tried to believe her, and did for a while. How long do you think the senior female can hold out? Sooner or later she's going to be forced to tell you who you are.

All day long, weeks on end sometimes, especially at the dinner table, the evening news while we ate, you were the evening news, the empty stares, the emptiness, that look went right through us. Where were you? *In the room but not in the room.* Bring your mind home. You're home most of the time, but you're almost never home.

We know that you love us, theoretically, but you make it hard, we include the senior female, to believe that you find us interesting. *(Love them in theory. Monk, monarch.)* In fact, we think that we bore you, we include the senior female. It would be helpful to the junior females, a little advice, Dad, we're speaking for ourselves, we haven't discussed this with the senior female, if you could manage a nice steady stream of chatter. Nice and steady, nice and attentive to us three, attend to us, smile like the weatherman, you know? You like acting, so act, once in a while do us a normal TV dad. Like on *The Brady Bunch*. Once in a while, Daddy. *Take them for ice cream, you all scream for ice cream.*

This thing of mine, these acts of self-annotation. "Annotation": a remark, a note, a commentary—on some passage of a book, intended to illustrate or explain its meaning, but the meaning never quite distilled, reason blocked *(yes),* preserving stories (the writer, his culture, his relations), meanings without ideas, flesh and blood, bleeding yourself and your loved ones and talking too much like yourself, like your children. To annotate passages in the book of myself, the senses of memory feeding greedily on myself. What did Stephen Crane say? Because it is bitter, and because it is my heart. *Stephen Crane is over the top. Two and six months, respectively. Respect that, put that in, explain it. Get the glossy self-pity out. And don't say: All for love, like a neoclassical soap. Say your own words. Do you have words of your own? Is that what's bothering you, buster? Tell us, what's your limit? Will you quote Shelley too? "I fall upon the thorns of life! I bleed!" Don't even think about it.* Annotation, writing about writing, the literary critic in an act of labor flowing from its hiding place, inside *elaboration.* It's what I do, don't make me say it's what I am.

I like the histories of words, their relatives, close, distant, and imaginary. I like Italian words, *si certo*! For example: *elaborare*. I like the annotation of annotation. Noun, from the Latin *annotatio: an,* to, and *notatio,* a marking, from *notare,* to mark. I have a relative, uncle by marriage, named *Notaro* (Antonio), close reader, marker of texts. At twelve I watched him from across the room, he was so thick-wristed, marking a racing form, half-listening to Puccini, shoeless and lounging, and Di Stefano (the tenor who ravishes me first) pouring it out. I associate the opera of nineteenth-century Italy with this raffish man named Notaro, vaguely criminal in manner, who does not read, or need, books. Intense textual concentration, pencil in a bone-crushing hand (he looked like Valentino), against a background of soaring lyric tenor.

I started to associate myself with the opera of nineteenth-century Italy at twelve, watching him, so engrossed, escaped from me, in the room but not in the room. Large Italian-American reading: concentrating for his freedom, happy.

My job is teaching (annotation from the mouth) and critical writing (annotation from the pen). "My job": hard for me to say those words. They had jobs. Anna Mary, my mother: the textile mills, then the assembly lines of General Electric. Wires, bits of metal, I don't know the names, she never taught me the names, small hard things with sharp edges, in bare hands, into radios. Frank John, my father: a painter, no, not that kind, with gallons, with brushes wider than my hand, thicker than my wrist, yielding overdeveloped forearms, still, nearing eighty.

One time, for an experiment, I referred to the room where I write, in my father's presence, as my "workroom." He said, "You referring to your library?" For twenty-six years it's rarely "How's work, Frank?" It's most of the time, "Frank, how's school?" If you never leave school, which I never did, maybe you never work. They generally don't say the desired words, not from scorn but from pride and glee, working-class style, believing (this is what they must believe) that the words I want are inadequate to their son's transcendence of their conditions. They don't say the word "transcendence." And I never say such words in their presence. Should university acquaintances come over when my parents are visiting, my parents tend to disappear (without preface) to their second-floor quarters because (this later, after the guests have gone) "We feel out of place, Frank." I don't say: Isn't this my house? Aren't you my parents? They were not permitted, by circumstances, beyond the eighth grade. And they do not require an explanation, nor an apology, for my life of physical ease, like a gentleman, like the son of a *padrone*. I don't say: Next time you escape upstairs, take me with you.

One time my father called our home a palace. He said it in Italian: *il palazzo*. That's a word. And where else should he live, this son like the son of a *padrone*? Who is not the son of a *padrone*. My father once told me, flatly, without resentment, why doesn't my father ever show resentment for the material conditions of his youth and middle age? I resent his lack of resentment, I don't know why. I want him to be angry. He never said "material conditions." He said, "When we were kids we ate a lot of bread to fill up our bellies." "When I married your mother," he said, "I was earning nine dollars a week." A fact. When he told me that, in the late 1950s, he was making forty-five a week. A 500 percent increase. He was amazed. I don't get paid by the week. The weak get paid by the week.

He never taught me to paint. They never talked to me about what they did on their jobs, as if the knowledge might tempt me, as if knowing the words could only bring me harm, like some communicable and fatal disease. "Go to school, Frank." They believe that if you find yourself in the working class you had better get out as fast as you can, if you can, if you know what's good for you. They live in Florida now, in a house which they bought cash. Before that they lived in their first home of their own, which my father bought when I was in college, then paid off in six years, in the middle sixties, when he was making in the middle sixties per week. We do not own the palace free and clear, and will not pay it off in six years.

One time, me and him, just between us. He: That's only mental, Frank. For Christ's sake, what if you had cancer? Me: silence. He: You know what I mean? Me: silence. He (never resentfully): You're a lucky man. In fact, I am a smashing success.

The more I went to school the more I became the stranger in the house. Which, of course, was the point. Which is what we all wanted, a gulf, the gulf made by their love, though we would never have thought to say it that way. My son the college teacher, et cetera. A number of pages back, I

was tough on T. S. Eliot for saying "to be educated above the
level of those whose social habits and tastes one has inherited
may cause a division within a man which interferes with happiness." What I said a number of pages back on Eliot is beginning to sound defensive, even to me.

The kitchen sink, me beside her, half her height: "Look
at my hands, like a man's hands, rough, touch my hands." My
hands are big and meaty, like my mother's except for the skin,
soft and smooth, perfect but for one outlandish writing callous on the left index (I do not type: my parents encouraged
in their firstborn, their son, no mechanical know-how. My
sister is another story). This writing callous is extraordinary,
changing a little in color lately, maybe it's a tumor, a melanoma, maybe, I'd better have it checked out. Can pens and
pencils be carcinogenic? Dad, I caught cancer from writing,
like a coal miner with black lung disease. I've got a real job,
and it entails risks. (In Italian, the words for tumor and honor
rhyme.) My hands are like the hands my mother wanted.
When she asked me to touch them, I did, I had to, but I didn't
like the feeling of my mother's hands. "Like" isn't the word;
I'm not going to say the right word. "Touch my hands,
Frankie."

The major theme at the kitchen sink was go to high
school and get good marks. The countertheme was, look at
my hands. My theme was, How come I won't keep on growing, Ma, right through the ceiling? How come I won't go
through the ceiling? I hear from her even now of their amuse-
ment, I posed endless impossible questions, then horror as I
took up arms against the sea of their diversionary answers,
driving wires and inserting things (not electrical plugs) into

electrical outlets, get that electricity out, naked, see the thing itself, a screwdriver straight up into a switched-on light bulb. A halo of sparks and a billion bits of eye-wrecking stuff, none of it touching me. Lucky even as a kid. Back then, I was perfect.

You used to drive us crazy, they say, and they say it as if they enjoyed it. My younger sister is, of course, another story. You know the story. I'm pretty sure she drove them crazy, but they never say to her, You used to drive us crazy, Elaine.

Frank's sister wasn't perfect. Your older brother. He's your older brother, Elaine. He gets away with everything. I've gotten away with murder.

At thirty-eight, he was able to afford his first car. At twelve, she had full responsibility for cooking for her parents and siblings, a family of eight. These things were never said directly to me. I gleaned them. And what shall the smashing success do for his kids comparable to what his parents did for him? He tells stories, directly to them, so that they will not have to glean them, of the slaughterhouse, at fourteen, and how frail he was at the time, his badge of honor, his bludgeon of honor. Before he developed a problem with sugar, you should have seen my father deal with ice cream. He was special when he dealt with ice cream. With a smile on his face I once saw him destroy an entire gallon of ice cream. Tell them that story.

Through me my parents triumphed over the circumstances of class. I didn't repeat their lives. Good. There could be no greater good. The American Dream, et cetera. But with me and my kids it's not a question of class. I don't know what it's a question of. What can I do to ensure that my kids won't repeat me? And how shall I envision my triumph as a father? Over the fatality of fatherhood. The fatal father. Whatever, it's only mental. We're lucky, me and my daughters. None of us has cancer yet, and I'm waiting for them, even now, but without need, fatally, they in their early twenties, to drive me crazy.

I imagine telling my parents that they're right, after graduate school I never got a job, I have been experiencing, instead, for twenty-six years, the onset of an illness. In obsolete usage (I'm not making this one up), an annotation is the first symptom of an illness. I could call myself an annotator, but prefer a usage the dictionary gives as rare: annotationist, one who practices, or is preoccupied with, or (I can't resist this extension) is a believer in annotations. To believe in annotation, hug it close, day and night. Annotationist as in contortionist. To practice and believe in contortions. To become what you believe ("I am a contortion"). As in exhibitionist ("I am an exhibition, on exhibition").

When does annotation become confession, confession carefully staged exhibitionism, unindicted co-conspirators in the autobiographical crimes of self-annotation? Memory and other crimes. Writing glosses on the self, laying on a glowing finish, enameling the dull surface of the abyss I am.

My father put glowing finishes on dull surfaces. He liked painting because it cleans things up, makes things better. Before it's too late, and without resentment, I'll tell my father that he's been writing all his life, that he, too, never had a job.

My mother did not find the assembly lines of General

Electric redemptive. Her work just depressed her, she came home depressed, her eyes puffed up like Robert De Niro in *Raging Bull,* looked like she'd been weeping for days.

He says that I don't have an illness. He says that I have a "racket" (as in organized crime). What, he says, two or three days a week, at most two hours a day? Four months off each year, no clock to punch, nobody looking over your shoulder, except yourself, and that's only mental, Frank. He's happy, his son beat the shit out of the system—the thought giving pleasure to the man who worked sometimes two shifts, weekends (almost always), so that we could have the things they couldn't have as kids, paying off the mortgage in six years.

We didn't see that much of each other. He didn't have access to the guilt-freeing idea of "quality time with your kids." He never had the time, I never had the time, Frank. In order that he be a good father, which he was. Without resentment. In order that I wouldn't repeat his life, which I haven't. Or was it that he needed to escape from us, this must be it, is this it?, become a monk of hard labor, finding his freedom there, happiness in backbreaking labor? His freedom. "You're laying on a high gloss, Dad, because you, too, worked all the time, you never had the time, even though you had the time, at the dinner table when you gave us the gaze, you never saw us, because you were revising sentences two shifts a day, weekends almost always, you couldn't let it go, you better let it go, you're escaping us, you wrote right over us without stopping, a hit-and-run writer, because you became your job, better clean the blood and hair off your pen, Dad, or the cops will get you. But if they get you don't worry, because you can call on us, as character witnesses, we will give truthful testimony as to your character."

"YOUR HONOR, I NEVER HAD THE TIME, EVEN THOUGH I HAD THE TIME. THERE WERE EXTENUATING CIRCUMSTANCES. AND SO ON."
"FRANK LENTRICCHIA, THIS COURT FINDS YOU PARTIALLY INNOCENT OF FATHERHOOD AND SENTENCES YOU TO REVISE YOUR SENTENCES FOR A PERIOD NOT TO EXTEND BEYOND YOUR FATHERHOOD."

As to my "character": from the Latin, a distinguishing mark (as in a system of writing); the Latin from the Greek, meaning an engraver's tool (derived from a verb meaning to engrave, to stamp). So: a mark of writing and an instrument for making marks of writing. Text and text-maker I am. A branding iron, for example, so much the better to burn FL into the flank-flesh of my kin, my memories. But this is not what they were referring to, my daughters, was it?, about which they shall give truthful testimony. The branded witnesses who will speak truthful testimony, as to my character, were not meditating etymologies.

I arrive in Ireland after an all-night flight, and an hour and a half of sleep, during which I never lose contact with the drone of the engines. Drive from Shannon to my destination, fighting sleep at the wheel on Irish roads, narrow and winding, great views every twenty seconds. *Take your eyes off the road, kill yourself for beauty.* Galway, my hotel, a little after midday, where I'll sleep it off, all afternoon, before meeting my host, Kevin Barry, at a nearby pub. I'll sleep like a log.

No sleep, none, the pub: Kevin's friends, two of whom are from the North, accents with built-in deviltry. One tells me days later that the other, who lives in Belfast, will, if I go up there to visit, arrange for my benefit a car bombing. He says, who barely knows me, "I think you might like that, Frank." I half-hope he's only half-joking, but I don't say anything because you never know, one thing leads to another, especially here. I'm not literally in favor of killing, if you know what I mean. I knock off two pints of stout.

Dinner at nine, wine-dark conversation, and wild Atlantic salmon, I cannot describe what that salmon did for me. I decide to go all the way, I have a brandy, which I almost never do. What the hell, I'll sleep late, I'll sleep it off. They're picking me up at ten for a drive out the Connemara Peninsula, mountains like arias. *They're* driving, what the hell, I'll sleep like a log. At the point of the brandy, it's one and a half hours out of thirty-six. Who cares, I'll sleep like death, I'll have two fucking brandies, and dream about my car exploding sky-high (arranged for my benefit, yes), a thing of beauty and a joy forever.

The hotel: crash-landing into the beautiful bed. Jet lag, twisting and turning, another one and a half hours. I see the dawn and it isn't rosy-fingered, the whites of my eyes are rosy-fingered, and all of a sudden it's almost 10:00 A.M., my God, they'll be here soon, but that's okay because *they're* driving on those Irish roads, I'll just drink up those views, I'll suck up those views. Three hours of sleep out of the last fifty.

Kevin arrives and all of a sudden I'm driving, too. Ten thousand kids are coming with us and we need all the cars we can get. We're joining a group of Irish historical geographers. Eventually we'll ferry off the Connemara Peninsula in the middle of nowhere to an island, Inishbofin (Island of the White Cow), where the historical geographers are going to read the rocks for us, and where one of them says, deadpan, "This is between three and seven thousand years old," at which point the literary critics, Kevin and me, who have to live with constant accusations of imprecision, give forth with snorts, like white cows.

Kevin's oldest son, Naoise, accompanies me on the way out. He's normal. I'm pretty normal. We have a normal conversation. The landscape is a megadose of caffeine.

We get to the place of the ferry. We've been driving for one and a half hours. The wind is worse than flying icicles, and if I don't buy a hat I'm going to freeze to death. Everyone has a hat but me and a kid named Luke (more about him later). The men tend to wear those kind, I don't know the name. I ask, What is the name? Nobody knows. It's the type they wear on golf courses in Ireland and Scotland and probably the other place in the vicinity whose name I don't want to mention in the same breath with Ireland ("I think you might like that, Frank"). You know the place, and you know the hat I mean. The one I buy is black and gray herringbone. This Irish hat is a terrific-looking thing, it's very sharp, it even looks terrific on me. I usually hate hats. With this hat I could—I think I look dangerous in this hat. I love this hat.

We walk around the island for two hours. Every once in a while one of the geographers gives an interesting little lecture which I don't pay any attention to. The kids are running around. This place is a little dangerous for kids, but the parents don't seem to notice. Kevin Barry is stepping over wet rocks with his baby in his arms, Rebecca, on steep hillsides, like it's no problem. Where is Rebecca's mother, Aoife? She was here just a minute ago.

Finally we eat lunch at a hotel on this island (I'm the type of person who, when it comes to meals, always says "finally"). It's been getting warmer by the minute, and no more wind, by the way. But I don't take off my terrific Irish hat. I put away three sandwiches (they weren't that big), a little salad, a pint of stout, a cup of tea, and some cake (it wasn't that rich), in my Irish hat. Three hours of sleep over the last fifty-six, and it's getting warmer by the minute.

We walk around for another two hours, geographers reading history in rocks, sediment, and a graveyard that goes back before Chaucer (on this last one I tune in). I assume all the walking is good for me, I'm at that age, you know?, and when we get back on the ferry I'm actually alive. I'm talking a streak about American universities, but I'm starting to stare, I'm starting to solidify, I'm becoming a rock. Standing on the ferry, I'm moving past sleep directly into death. In exactly ninety-four seconds this ferry will explode sky-high and our bodies will wash ashore on the Island of the White Cow, where birds feed upon us, and our bones, picked clean, become pearls between three and seven thousand years old. And Luke alone, who doesn't have a hat, survives to tell all. Our pearly skeletons, says Luke, look funny in our Irish hats.

Back to the cars. I have to drive on a narrow and winding two-lane road for an hour and a half, all the way back to

Galway. This is not good. But the worst is yet to come. They descend upon me. All of a sudden I'm popular with kids. I know it's my car, a model recently introduced into Ireland, brand new and terrific-looking, but the kids cover the truth well. They just say they want to come back with me. (Have they come back with me because of the car or because they love me? Two weeks later, deep into another dinner, and much wine, the amused Kevin Barry will put this very question.) Four of them pile in:

> Luke Feeney, age twelve, of Dublin
> Ruth Barry, age eleven, of Dublin
> Simon Feeney, age eight, of Dublin
> Tristram Ryder, age five, of Galway
> Frank Lentricchia, age fifty-one, the driver, an American

What does this list sound like to you? Where do you see lists like this? You know what I'm saying. Why did those parents let those kids get in the car with me, on those Irish roads, driving on the wrong side, I don't give a shit what they call it, it's the wrong side, with this tired American (tired isn't the word), this hit-and-run writer? I desire to absolve myself of all responsibility, but I don't know how to do it. How do you get away with something like that?

These kids are brilliant, they mention the car not even once. Tristram Ryder, age five, of Galway—I'm glad I don't have that name: who could live up to that name? Tristram Ryder doesn't say a word. He sleeps all the way, having nightmares about his name. The other three, sensing the truth of my condition, boldly take matters into their own hands.

They decide that what I require more than anything else is intellectual stimulation, spiced by seductive references to my hat. Luke, a terrific-looking devil, described by Kevin as an "opera star," a "wild man," and a "completely responsible baby-sitter," assumes his proper position on my left, in the front passenger's seat, and immediately informs me that my hat is "grand." Then he cleverly ups the ante: "You look grand in your hat, Frank. You look Irish now. Might you be Irish, Frank?"

These Irish kids, they invented charm, they say your name a lot in conversation, knowing you like that, they caress your name every time they say it, *but I am The Pied Piper of Galway, and I have come to teach their parents a lesson. I'll steal these abandoned children, who shouldn't be driving with me. I'll open up a mountain, I'll drive right in, then I'll close it up and they'll never be seen again, and we'll listen forever to soaring bel canto arias, totally absorbed, escaped from each other, inside the mountain.*

I was in a dangerous state. Those parents should have known. Somebody will have to testify as to their character, and it won't be their kids, because they'll never see their kids again. Those poor kids couldn't resist my hat, they never had a chance.

The others *(but not Tristram Ryder, who'll never know what hit him, who'll wake up inside the mountain, where he's doomed to spend the rest of his days, listening to soaring bel canto arias, which he doesn't much care for, which he might get used to if I let him wear the terrific hat, which once in a while I will)*, the others, Ruth and Simon, chime in every once in a while with "Might you be Irish, Frank?" Their voices, of course, are sincere.

The wild man, out of the blue, proposes that we determine the average age of "the humans inside the car." I'm hoping he's including me in the crucial category and I do a mind-bogglingly quick computation and announce, authoritatively, that we are collectively a little under eighteen, a figure I love, until the opera star says, cheerfully—*but he'll become my trusted elder son, inside the mountain my inheritor*—in this instance, he says, the devil!, the average is a "shade misleading, don't you think, Frank?" *(But inside the mountain he'll respect my age, he'll shield me, child of my left hand, from all references to my age, and at the grave site will deliver an elegy of his own composition, more witty than sad.)* I change the subject fast and ask them, since they're all studying Irish (which they dislike having to do), if someone can tell me my name in Irish. The inventive Simon comes forward quickly with "Frunc," a perfect description of my inner life of the moment. What difference could it make that "Frunc" wasn't Irish, that Frank doesn't exist in Irish? "Frunc" wasn't any language but Simon's, but what difference does that make? I saw my Irish hat in a Dublin store. I went in and asked them the name. They told me. I wish that I hadn't gone in.

Eyes wide, how many times? for micro-seconds, I lose consciousness. I could have killed those kids, *and I am The Pied Piper of Galway, and they are not the kids who get stolen at the end, they're the rats. "Would you be thinking we're rats, Frank?" "Don't you love us, Frank?" Taking them over the brink, their parents should have known, they should have protected their kids, that's what they were supposed to do, that's why they were parents.*

Frunc the zombie, I can hardly talk, but these kids do not intend to let me kill them. They jolt me with agile leaps of disputation. The Los Angeles riot (the first topic), divorce,

Catholicism, and the alleged celibacy of priests (they do not mention nuns), an East European soccer star whose name they say every so often, connected to nothing (a charm, no doubt, against their driver's unsoundness), the Provisional IRA (they say they know someone involved, they could introduce me), television network news, the restaurant scene in Galway (they caution against the Italian restaurant), and abortion (Ruth nobly holding feminist ground against Luke's reactionary thrusts). They do not ask me if I believe that abortion constitutes murder of the unborn, and Frunc does not volunteer his incoherent views. He would not tell them that his incoherence is a function of his present stupefaction because to do so would be to lie, *and I desire to absolve myself of all responsibility, but I don't know how to do it. How do you get away with something like that?*

I'm writing these last pages in Dublin. I think I might call those Dublin kids. We could go to the zoo. Or I might not.

I wonder if they sell ice cream at this zoo, which they say is the second-oldest in Europe. I can really put it away, I can eat ice cream with the best. It's one of my extremes. I wonder how much those kids could put away? A lot, but probably not as much as me. Probably those three Dublin kids together going all out couldn't put away as much as me.

It's possible that I am the emperor of ice cream. Or maybe it's my father. One of us. It couldn't be both because you can't have two emperors, and because there's a difference between me and my father. Men of ice cream. Men of ice. Which will thaw first?

I might not call those Dublin kids because maybe we've escaped from each other. It's not necessarily cowardly, not to call. You have to consider what you're escaping from; you have to consider that very carefully before making a final judgment. The subject is freedom. Theirs and mine.

Those Dublin kids, Luke, Ruth, and Simon. Whose children are they? They might be deeply shocked, they might even be traumatized by what the Ice Cream Monster can do to ice cream. Kids can only take so much. It wasn't me, it was them. They were the Pied Piper.

Imaginary Irish fatherhood, it's delightful. Try it: you have nothing to lose except your real family.

8

Will you, I pray, demand that demi-devil
Why he hath thus ensnar'd my soul and body?
— *OTHELLO,* V, II

My country is getting ready to celebrate the Fourth of July, and I'm going to tell you about how I imagine taking my vengeance upon a stranger, for what I saw this stranger do in a bar, in Durham, North Carolina, late on the evening of November 22, 1963. This is the fantasy:

I see myself engaged in painstaking research, a skill I honed as a graduate student at Duke University in the early sixties; expending considerable portions of my funds, which are by no means bottomless; yielding fully to my obsession, which requires no honing. Then I find him at last, living in a perfectly kept fifties ranch-style home, in every city in America where I've lived or passed through since the evening of November 22, 1963.

When I arrive, at 2:00 A.M., he is asleep on his back, fully naked, his great spreading belly covering his knees. He weighs between 800 and 1,000 pounds. I lean over and whisper in his ear: Ask not what your country can do for you, ask what you can do for your country. I whisper: *Ich bin ein Berliner.* Out of the black part of my soul, I whisper: Has anyone here seen my old friend John?

I cannot see his existence, his belly hides his existence, not that I wanted to see his existence. Who would want to see his existence? Much less make love to it. It would take his immensest effort, and then he would likely fail, even with the tips of his fingers, to caress his existence. And I lean over and I whisper: So you'll no more go a–masturbating. Shall I cut off your existence?

He awakes, but I do not bother to tell him that death has apparently been confirmed, that I had recently seen on CNN the autopsy photos. I do not bother to tell him that with half his brains blown out, the other half removed by a team of specialists in forensic medicine, and with that hole in his throat, which those efficient bastards in Dallas had made worse with a tracheotomy, putting their knives into it, wounding the wound, and with those eyes of nothing anymore, wide open to the ceiling, the harsh lights fixing their beams upon his paleness, young Jack was still a handsome man. And there were, I don't bother to tell him, because he must not know what passion is, how many women and (oh yes) how many men who loved and wanted him, God knows, and in their grief would have been happy to, yes God knows, even right then and there, that grievous night at Bethesda Naval Hospital.

I stand at the foot of his bed, attired in a sleeveless white gown of grand flowing folds, sporting an expensive Afro toupee, my skin darkened in the tanning beds to a commanding and gleaming swarthiness, my large gold earring glinting in the fierce arc lamp that I bring here for this occasion, for this, his final entertainment, brilliant light sculpting me out of the darkness, a statue, a photograph, a movie, an opera, and I say, huskily, as his eyes open, Desdemona, the time has come to consummate our marriage. He nods, he winks, he says: I just dreamt of Kennedy, that nigger-lover who got what he wanted. Good buddy, you've changed, you're starting to look like some kind of religious nigger, you sure are. In response, I croon out of the black part of my soul, Has anyone here seen my old friend Martin? And then I say, I am the multicultural avenger, the black Italian-American Othello, and in my aspect you behold all that is best of dark and bright. Quick, make clean your loins, for Othello has found his occupation. And now he knows (oh, yes, God is real), he knows at last that he has met a serious character (yes, Jesus, the road has been rough).

Without another word, I part the folds of my flowing white gown at the center of my torso, at the still point of the turning world, and expose to him my existence. I say, pointing to my existence, Do you know what this is? He replies, quickly, but with respect, Good buddy, that's your penis. And I say, No, this is not my penis, this is love. Then I say, Do you know who Othello is? And he replies, quickly, but softly, Yes, an old-fashioned Negro. And I say, Good, you're getting better, but it will do you no good. It is too late. Do you know what Othello means in Irish? Silence, puzzlement. And I say, in Irish Othello signifies handsome young Jack Kennedy who comes dripping in his brains in the middle of the night to make love to thousand-pound men. Then I remove it from the case I have hidden under his bed, an interesting instrument, and hold it high before him. And I say, Behold, do you know what this is? He says, softly, That's a saw. I say, No, try again. He says, A chain saw, good buddy? And I say, No, no, it's a *Texas* chain saw. Then I say, Darling, *mia piccina,* your superb warrior is now strapping this interesting instrument to the end of his loving existence. Big guffaw, followed by a strangled sound, as he sees me, hands at my hips, watching it, my strapped-on Texas chain saw, rising, thanks be to the generous Lord, twelve o'clock high, it is risen.

I consider telling him some of the reasons, ah, the foreplay of reasons, which are infinite in number. I consider telling him why no one will crawl in passion upon his autopsy table. I consider pointing to my loving existence, with its interesting extension, my existence *dentata,* yes, and saying, You are, are you not, a racist cocksucker? It is good to overcome prejudice. Suck on this. I consider saying, I have come to tell you all: I watched you that night, drunk, two hundred and twenty pounds of sloppy brutality, happy, mocking the tapes running over and over on the TV above the bar, mocking Jack's gestures and accent, the happiest man in the world, and me, a hundred and fifty pounds of skinniness, with no chance to do to you what needed to be done, you would have done it to me; and through the sixties, every night in bed, yes, this is true, motherfucker, I saw myself in the presidential limousine in Dealey Plaza, taking the bullets in the back of the head, every night, then much later, in the eighties, I saw the Zapruder film for the first time and I had to change my narrative, I had to take it from the front, my brains blown back, Jackie fetching my blown brains and Reagan, smug, saying in California, the morning after Bobby, "Political opportunists come to our great state and stir people up, then these things happen," and that dumb shit who could have got one from your side, but she forgot to put a bullet in the chamber, Christ, she was point blank, and don't tell me Ford is nice, Ford pardoned Nixon, fuck Ford, and that other dumb shit who also could have got one from your side, he could have gotten Reagan himself but he used a stupid .22, why didn't he use a .357 Magnum? Reagan needed another face-lift, didn't he? and don't tell me Reagan is dumb but has a good heart, because fuck Reagan's heart and fuck the colon cancer which he beat and fuck the skin cancer which was never anything in the first place, skin cancer is bullshit unless it's a melanoma which he never had totally out of control on his face. I am told you can get a melanoma in the eye. Have you been told that? You want the final straw? This asshole Bush who thinks he can vomit on international television with impunity, the Japanese laughed at that asshole, who can blame them? and someone is going to have to answer for Medgar and for Malcolm and for Martin and for those children in that church basement in Birmingham, September 15, 1963, because don't let me get started on what happens to blacks, I'll never finish. Not all the Kennedy pain, which is great, and not all the white pain in America, which is no question not small, can ever equal black pain in America. Someone from your side definitely must answer, and I don't mean in the next world, because this is the fucking next world, we have too long forborne, but now our forbearance is gone and we don't want Quayle, obviously we won't take Quayle, and don't mention George Wallace because we're not stupid, because we don't think George counts, because those suits of his that look like he bought them at K mart show us there is good in George.

But I tell him nothing. Because knowledge, no matter how grim, always uplifts, because reasons will give him confidence in an order of things, will tell him that he is part of a sweeping narrative, will convince him that his fate is luminous, and I do not wish to give this man the consolation of reason. Most of all, I do not want him to know how much I still miss Jack, I do not want him to know how much Jack's death robbed me of myself.

So I tell him nothing, so I give him no reason, so my fantasy dries up, as he nods, as he winks, as I stand before him costumed and adorned, as he spreads wide his arms, as he begins to look like an Italian-American character in a long-running TV series, as he says, Frank, hey, *paesan,* long time no see, *paesan,* for Christ's sake put on your regular clothes, Frank. Frank, be yourself for a change, come on now, you think I don't know? *Me?* You think I don't know? Get over here and give me a big hug, you fuckin' chooch. Frankie, John Kennedy is dead.

August–December 1992

Light the first light of evening . . .   —WALLACE STEVENS

Try not to jump to the conclusion that I'm having a problem just because I tell you this is my second attempt at an ending, three and a half months later. Don't think that the writer is in agony, and so forth, not even if I say this is my eighth attempt, three and a half months after it ended. I wrote the first ending in late August '92. It was brief (less than two pages), it was semicryptic, it was heavy with literary gesture. I believe that the point of the August '92 ending was to evade what happened in late August, what was happening all summer long.

"Ending": that's a word I like, very much. It feeds my desire for continuing presence. An "ending," the end that doesn't want to end. You know how some people talk about it? They were there, you weren't. They're not telling you that you missed something. They're not trying to include you, who cares about you? They're in love, they can't get over it, they're still in there, and they're not going to let it end, because they refuse to be dragged back down into their selves. That's what they're telling you, and they tell *you* only because they have to tell somebody. These people live in some transported realm, inside the act and scene of their coming. They'll explode if they don't express themselves, so they pour it out, in an act of pure telling, the coming again of the coming. Who doesn't like coming? They believe that they have to have perpetual orgasm. Or else. Some of them are writers; the rest need to become writers. Psychoanalytical types tell us these people have a death wish. Theological types say it's their desire for God. The aesthetes say pleasure. The pleasure God Death. Mr. Death. I don't know what I would say. I'll say this: I have long suspected myself of being one of these people.

In August '92 I could see at last, I needed to see, the *end* of my book on modernism, eight years in the making, and for what? The most consistently painful writing I'd ever done, it was relentless, and for what? I couldn't contain the pain of that work and she took it. I used that pain like a meat cleaver, I hacked away, I expressed myself. About ten years ago, I stopped reading literary criticism. All those years, those books I did, and now what? I'm not yet an old man (he says), and I should be exploring. My lengthy c.v., the chaired professorship, the receding hairline, I check it every morning. Let my book on modernism *end*. Let me stop writing literary criticism, let that *end*. But then what? Don't let *this* end, whatever this is.

I don't believe in God, that's obvious to me, who is planning his third trip, in eighteen months, to a Trappist monastery, but it's also obvious to me that I'm praying, I'm writing this, the end again, good, what seemed finished in August is not yet finished, very good, an ending now unfolding with me inside the process, this book of writings of myself, writing my selves. Let these multiple acts of writing, let them be without end. Amen. I prefer to stay inside; I want to be this. You know "this"? This activity. These selves. Writings.

The fact encrypted inside the August '92 ending concerned my marriage. My marriage became this fact. Legal documents impossible to understand, amicable agreements of maximum mutual understanding and stunning generosity, because we are decent people. The division of community property, without acrimony, because who's better than us? You take that rug even though it's worth four hundred times more than all the other rugs put together, because you love that rug. No more discussion, at least we won't have to discuss this shit anymore, these conversations are killing me. Me too. No more conversation. Yes, now we can be kind. No more talking, Christ Almighty, who wants to talk to you? You'll be the first person I'll date. Oh yeah? Who'll be the second? You're telling lies about us. Who's telling lies? In your book. I'm not lying, goddamn it. They'll like you in your book, you killer. Who's a killer? You. Me? You calling me a killer? Yes. How many killers live in this house, let me ask you that? Because I'm not the only one, Jesus fucking Christ Almighty, I'm not the only one. Who said you were the only one? Fuck that rug, fuck it.

I am the only one here. Jesus is not here. His name is no longer spoken here. This silence is not angry. This depression is amicable. I'm skating on thin ice, but the ice is not going to break, the problem is that the ice is not going to break. Nothing will happen. The fucking ice holds forever. And now what? Nothing, that's what, nothing.

A legal separation in North Carolina means that everything is done that must be done except you have to wait a year from the day you sign the legal separation papers, and then somebody, not even the lousy lawyer, some clerk, files a piece of paper and you probably pay 500 dollars (not to the clerk but to the lousy lawyer, the clerk could use it), and then you're divorced. It's all over. I don't know how much they'll charge but they'll charge too much. I'll write a check for the whole amount because she'll forget her checkbook, which she apologizes for, then she touches my arm just above the elbow, and when she gets home to her own home where she's lived for a year by herself and with one of our cats, we divided the cats, she took the one who loved her, the male, I took the one who loved me, the female, we were having affairs with our cats, that's why we broke up, she writes a check and then drives immediately to the post office. Or it's the other way around. Except I forget the checkbook on purpose. I don't know why I pull this trick. Except I don't touch her on the arm just above the elbow. Or anywhere else. Because I'm not sentimental. She's sentimental. That's why we broke up, it wasn't the cats. I don't do sentimental. We'll split the final fee. Suddenly I touch her arm just above the elbow and we immediately decide to call off the whole thing. Let's call the whole thing off. Telling lies in my book. Jesus Christ, unend the end.

I didn't mention the words "legal separation" in the August '92 version of the ending, but neither did I evade the fact those words refer to. I think it was pretty clear, in that version, what the story was. The fact that I evaded, buried out of sight, under guilty literary gesture, was the summer's counterfact: I had been working well as it was all going down, and now one of us is going, the movers are here, they're nice, I like them even though one of them gouges my wall, he didn't do it on purpose, did he? or did he?, let them take their time, these guys are first-class, today we live in a racially integrated home, goodwill is much in evidence in our home today. I don't write *while* the movers are here, because I'm not sick. After they go, out of respect for the situation, I don't do a couple of nice revisions I have in my head. I'll do them tomorrow. I won't forget because I'll think about them while the movers are here. I'll fix them in my mind. Then I'll do them tomorrow. In my home, I'll write the new phrases into the text, and I'll like them.

In early September, when the actual physical separation took place, I was launched into the writing that would become the opening section of this book, this writing is unleashed, and the passive voice is right, because I can't claim to be the unleasher, I am the unleashee, it's some Higher Power, and it pours forth, the best time I've ever had as a writer. I became a surfer of infinite finesse, carried by a wave of inexhaustible power, the Higher Power of the Wave God of Writing.

I figure out the psychology of what's going on even as it goes on, because what do you think? I'm stupid?, but knowing what I know does not diminish my pleasure. This knowledge enhances it. This self-consciousness is thrilling. In September, when the physical separation, and, you know, the writing, the exuberance. And don't call it escape. There are better words. Friends say I look good. You've changed. Frank, you look better than you have in years. Some motherfucker declares me a pleasure to be with. Some asshole. They come to the conclusion that this separation is good for me. They're right. A couple of them say this conclusion out loud in front of me. I haven't yet said, because now I'm such a pleasure to be with, I'm going to separate you from your life, and then you'll look better than you have in years, you'll be a pleasure to be with.

In fact, one thing alone is good for me. Everything else is bad only when this is not happening. You know "this"? When this is happening nothing is bad, I can stand anything, I can take their best shot, they nail me with their best shot and I don't go down, I feel no pain, I'm anesthetized. I like my disease very much. God of Writing, let me embrace it. God of Writing, let me not call it a disease. Is it true? Never friends? Eighteen years?

There's more dust in this house now and I don't like it (the dust, not the house, okay sometimes the house too), it doesn't get cleaned as often as when you know who used to clean it, who used to live here, in my home. Sometimes I clean it. I'm excellent at cleaning. I'm her equal at cleaning.

I'm eating out too much, not that I can't afford it. I'm eating out too much. I just got through Thanksgiving and now here comes Christmas, which I'll spend with my parents in Florida. Four days in Florida. I better bring at least three books. My parents like to go to the movies with me. I'll insist on paying. My father will resist, but I'll win. We'll go to two movies. I'll bring this to Florida. I'll look at my watch a lot. Didn't I tell you not to jump too quick? I always look at my watch a lot, that's who I am, an escapee from the present. I never liked the holidays. Therefore, this holiday season is no different. It's only logical. It's no different. My mother will cook magnificently, she always does, and then, of course, she will denigrate her own cooking. She won't listen to me. I'll go to bed on the early side. Try not to jump. I had thirty-six plates of lasagna. Thirty-six plates, Ma. That proves how good. She says: Naturally, you're my son, that's why thirty-six plates. The lasagna is no good. How come you barely touched your salad? What's wrong with my salad that you barely touched it? I'm not having sleeping problems, and my nightmares are traditional, except for one, and my parents never gave me a hard time. Never. They'll find me a semi-pleasure to be with.

Nobody will bring it up. You don't think I'm going to bring it up, do you? Then all of a sudden my mother brings it up. I start to stutter and stumble, because I have nothing to say. What am I supposed to say? I'm sad? Is that what the fifty-two-year-old son says to the eighty-year-old parents? He says: "I'm sad." They smile, they say: "Don't worry. The fucking ice is going to hold forever." My father comes to the rescue. He says, "Ann, for God's sake" (we pray a lot in our family) "if he wants to bring it up he'll bring it up. Why do you have to bring it up? If he wants to bring it up he'll bring it up." My father does not bring it up because he does not wish to cut out his own heart. He believes that we will be saved by the silence. By "we" I mean him and me. My mother believes that the talking will save us, the three of us. They loved her (why did I write the past tense?) and they'll never see her again. And try not to tell me it's not out of the question that they'll see each other again. I know it's not out of the question. I'm not stupid. They'll never see her again. She'll make a phone call to the one who is left, after the other one dies. I'll tell you who's stupid. Rational people, that's who. Their deaths will crush her.

I'll bring a big biography of Kafka to Florida. Kafka in Florida. This book will enable me to relive my autumn redemption, when I rediscovered myself as a teacher. Along with the literary criticism, I thought that the teaching was gone too. Good thing it wasn't. I had a beautiful time in that class. My students' faces told me that they did, too. Or maybe they thought I was crazy. One hundred students and only two sleepers. I lectured on Mondays and Wednesdays—it was nonstop cavorting—and my teaching assistants took smaller groups on Fridays for discussion, I hope not of my madness. ("For ten points, describe with three words the quality of Professor Lentricchia's derangement.") Yeats, Joyce, Conrad, Kafka, Eliot, Stevens, Fitzgerald, Faulkner. We had amorous engagements on Mondays and Wednesdays. Kafka I had never taught before. Kafka, the first time. A hot new lover. ("Professor Lentricchia is a literary homosexual necrophiliac.") Franz, yes Franz Oh Francis yes yes.

On several occasions my students must have thought I was talking about myself through the material. (Tory says to Tuck: "When you go to his office hours, which I dare you to do, bring a gun." Tuck says: "I already thought of that, Tory, what do you think? I'm stupid?") Do anything to keep them rapt, then nail them. I didn't work hard to cover it up, except with Kafka. I didn't quote to them this letter of Kafka's which I might have written: ". . . literary work was my one desire, my single calling. . . . But the wish to portray my own inner life has shoved everything into the background; everything else is stunted, and continues to be stunted. . . . Often, I am seized by a melancholy though quite tranquil amazement at my own lack of feeling . . . that simply by consequence of my fixation upon letters I am everywhere else uninterested and in consequence heartless."

When I came across this letter my first reaction was, This is the best interpretation of this new work of mine that I can imagine. Franz Kafka, my kinsman. My impulse was to make it the epigraph for the whole thing. Then a friend, to whom I read the quotation over the phone, a long-distance call, asked me a question which gave me pause. He said: What percentage of the time is it true? I said: What do you mean? I knew what he meant. He said: Seventy percent? Why did he pick such a high percentage? I said: Sometimes it feels like a hundred percent but I hope not. Then he suddenly changed the subject before I could ask *him* the percentage question, which I was eager to do, considering that I was talking to a committed writer. I didn't want to admit that I got the point of the percentage question: Don't like Kafka's letter too much. He exaggerates. Besides, his feelings of heartlessness are an occupational hazard, they're natural, so live with them. Besides, he was covering up something. Frank, we tend to cover up.

Franz Kafka, my kinsman, the jerk-off artist of Prague, that's who he must have thought he was, because to write as he wrote, in constant self-meditation, called constantly inward by his single desire, is selfish. It's inconsiderate. Shockingly so. But during the act, he loses his self. Was it selfish of him to want to lose himself? Was he supposed to apologize for losing it? Later, in the grip of the enemy, when his self came back, he practiced the deeper form of self-abuse, self-loathing. He felt heartless and the feeling was unappeasable, because Kafka was not a reasonable man. But during the act of writing (this was his secret), he felt careless. During was good, even when it was difficult.

So he convicted himself a cold-blooded bastard, just because he was committed, 100 percent. He didn't get married. You have to give him that. Did he kill somebody? Did he rape? Molest children? Did he rob from the poor? He was committed not out of choice but because he was who he was. He couldn't have changed even if he tried, and he didn't try. I'm glad he didn't try. So he felt melancholy. But he felt something else, too, which he almost buried out of sight, from shame. At times, freedom from emotional agitation. At times, surpassing serenity in a calm beyond calm. He felt, but only at times for Christ's sake, a peace that he must have believed others did not feel, he thought he had gone directly to heaven, and he wondered what he had done to deserve it. And so he beat himself up regularly in order to ensure that he did not feel the peace too often. And he didn't.

The quotation from Kafka wouldn't work as an epigraph because it doesn't tell enough truth, it evades too well the scandal of aesthetic pleasure, the last frontier. I wouldn't have lifted a finger to help Kafka change his point of view. I like too much what came from his misery.

Next fall, when I teach the course again, I must start with the Kafka letter. Or should I spring it on them next week for the final exam? An identification question. Who wrote this? Ninety-eight say Kafka. The two sleepers say, You did, shithead. You wrote everything in this course. That's why we slept. Finish your book on modernism before it's too late.

Kafka wrote a story called "A Hunger Artist," about a circus performer whose act consists in marathon fasting, who eventually starves himself to death. "A Hunger Artist" is K's great pose and cover-up, his parable of the compulsive artist who only suffers. I wish he had acted upon another desire as well, the guiltiest of all his desires, to write "The Lasagna Artist." It would have been a parable of irreducible ecstasy, and don't call it masturbation. I think I could have helped him to do it, if I could have taken him to a movie I saw just last week, Federico Fellini's *Intervista*. I want him to write "The Lasagna Artist" because he's getting tired of that same old voice of his and he's looking for something new, and if they cure his tuberculosis he's not going to die at forty-one, he's going to live a long time, maybe until fifty-two, he's going to have to change that voice once in a while or he's going to bore himself to death. So what'll he do, at fifty-two, old Franzeroo? Thirty-six plates? And the salad too?

Intervista, "interview." Just for us. Fellini, in his seventies, offering us his creativity, taking us on a tour of his life in art—producers, clowns, set designers, actors, the technology and all the machinery, the smell of the greasepaint. This tour plucks your mind out, and we can't tell the difference between real and imaginary, documentary and fiction, and we don't care. There's one of Fellini's abandoned projects, your novel *Amerika,* abandoned, Franz, *abbandonato*! Let's celebrate this, his festive meal, his life in the process of making his art as his art, as his true life. Let's celebrate with gusto, for he has nothing to say. Except: I am doing this. Forget who I am outside this doing this, for which I have no name. Because this is serious, because this is how I love. With apologies to my family, I offer you my bliss. Without apologies.

I remember taking my parents on one of those Hollywood studio tours, years ago. In the middle of it, my father, who's about Fellini's age, shook his hand in a quintessential Italian gesture which I cannot describe with justice, and he said, "*Madon',* Frank, the fakery!" He loved that tour, especially when he said, "*Madon',* Frank, the fakery!"

ABOUT THE AUTHOR

FRANK LENTRICCHIA is the author of several contro-
versial and acclaimed books, including *After the New
Criticism, Criticism and Social Change,* and *Ariel and
the Police*. He is the Katherine Everett Gilbert Professor of Literature at Duke University.

ABOUT THE TYPE

This book was set in Bembo, a typeface based on an old-style Roman face that was used for Cardinal Bembo's tract *De Aetna* in 1495. Bembo was cut by Francisco Griffo in the early sixteenth century. The Lanston Monotype Machine Company of Philadelphia brought the well-proportioned letter forms of Bembo to the United States in the 1930s.